PSST!!
Wanna Know a Secret?

Getting Smarter, Making More Money

Things They Didn't Teach You in School

By
JClark

© 2016 Joseph F. Clark
Saint Augustine, FL

All rights reserved. No part of this book shall be reproduced, stored in a retrieval system, or transmitted by any means without the written permission of the publisher.

International Standard Book 13: 978-1-60452-120-7
International Standard Book 10: 1-60452-120-1
Library of Congress Control Number: 2016905919

BluewaterPress LLC
52 Tuscan Way Ste 202-309
Saint Augustine FL 32092
www.bluewaterpress.com

This book may be purchased online at –
www.bluewaterpress.com/psst

Please note that address information is subject to change. At the time of printing, the address was correct, but may have changed since. Please check our website for the latest address information for BluewaterPress LLC.

Contents

List of Tables	xi
Introduction	xiii
A note for the Parents	xvii
The argument for staying in school	xxiii
Chapter 1 – The schools may have failed you	1
Chapter 2 - Self-assessment	9
Chapter 3 – Choices	13
Chapter 4 – The cool apartment	19
Chapter 5 – Your grocery bill and clothes	31
Chapter 6 - Your budget	35
Chapter 7 – You need a job	41
Chapter 8 – Got to have wheels	45
Chapter 9 – You have to save	55
Chapter 10 – Credit and credit cards	63
Chapter 11 – Identity Theft	71
Chapter 12 – Job? Or career?	79
Chapter 13 – Are you ready for college?	87
Chapter 14 – The military option	93
Chapter 15 – Leadership & Attitude	101
Chapter 16 – The big bucks	105
Chapter 17 – Keeping your nose clean	115

List of Tables

Table 1. Basic survival budget	21
Table 2. What it's really going to cost.	24
Table 3. A more realistic monthly budget.	37
Table 4. Year-end balance and interest paid.	65

Introduction

For the last 26 years, I have enjoyed teaching young people on the college level. Before that, I taught all kinds of people how to fly. My graduate degree is a master of aeronautical science with a specialization in aviation education. While in the Navy, one of the billets I held was that of the squadron training officer, a position in which I was responsible for keeping track of and planning the training of everyone in the unit. Making complex things seem simple for those who do not quite understand fascinates me, along with the process of teaching itself.

I have also been observant, trying to understand why things happen the way they do with our newest and latest generations. The children of friends have been a curious study. Some have really impressed me. Wherever they fall on the scale, today's youth are a very interesting and diverse group.

I have concerns for our young people. In my position, I have had the chance to work with some of the brightest and gifted of students. In public, I have come across many young people who are very bright, but unfortunately, they are not getting a fair deal when it comes to education. Schools are overcrowded, teachers overtasked, and there are too many disruptive troublemakers in many classrooms. Consequently, learning is degraded in such environments.

The truly gifted will find success. They are the doctors, lawyers, teachers, engineers, and scientists of the future. They get it. Those who don't get it are the timid children with good intellect, but who are too quiet to make their voices heard.

This book is for them.

In many cases, I see their potential, but sometimes it is hidden, sometimes hidden deep. Of these young people, I also see their reluctance to do things in the accepted ways of the past. I can see they get it, but not quite. I am also aware of their enthusiasm for learning, coupled with a sincere desire to figure out life—on their terms.

Our youth, as "us kids" did in the past, tend to reject the ideas, methods, and the ways of previous generations. It is common in nature, to reject the ideas of the parents. I soon discovered it was easier to listen and follow the instructions of "the older folk" and swim with the flow, rather than fight the current.

One thing I have seen in our educational system is that many students are taught to read in a way that destroys almost all potential for reading enjoyment. Some teachers make students read material the students dislike. In such cases, the lesson reinforced is the idea that reading is boring—instead of the concept that reading is an exciting adventure from which one can learn much. Reading, for those who mastered it, is an exciting adventure from the first page of a book, to the last. Sadly, many of our youth today rarely read more than a couple of paragraphs at a time—and then, only while on the Internet.

On occasion, I have come across youngsters who really remind me of my younger self. I find I want to help those young people, to give them a few ideas, to let them know about some of the secrets I have discovered along the way. I also know that if I say something outright, there is a good chance they will reject the idea out of hand right away. Young people, when presented a new idea or information, must feel some form of ownership of that idea. To this end, I will just let them "discover" this little book—maybe it will be left somewhere by someone concerned for their future. Then they can actually decide whether to read it or not.

Students need to know that those who read will develop ideas that will help them become successful. It is, as pointed out in later pages, their choice.

I want to thank many people who have influenced me along my path. There were many teachers, friends, peers, flight instructors, doctors, lawyers—all who eventually became my friends and contributed much to this energy called my life.

First, I wish to thank my wife, Ardis, for her continued support and excellent proofreading skills. I also need to thank Mike Holoman, for contributing ideas and catching errors in the original manuscript.

Then, there is my "Uncle Buddy," Marcus M. Woodham, Jr. He gave me great guidance throughout much of my life.

And of course, my mom, Elizabeth Vadella Woodham Clark, who gave me an inquisitive mind, taught my sister, two brothers, and me how to read, introduced us to logic, and helped with many word problems.

A note for the Parents

This is an important book for your children. This is especially true if you want to help your children succeed beyond high school. You may define their success as graduation from high school. Or you might think success only comes with a college degree. Maybe you have a completely different concept of success; still, the question becomes, where are *they* going after graduation?

Take a look at your children, a truly objective look. What do you see? Are you content with your children merely graduating from high school and getting into the workforce? Do you want them to attend college? Do you want them to enter a professional field? Can you see them creating their own business, becoming successful, and happy?

When discussing the education of our children, there's something a few parents realize more than others. Our educational system is broken. There is much literature written about the system that explains the existence of two systems: one in the rural and suburban areas, the other in the inner cities. Unfortunately, both systems are broken. One more so than the other.

Martin L. Gross, author of *The Conspiracy of Ignorance: The Failure of American Public Schools*, (Harper Perennial; 1st edition, September 5, 2000), makes an interesting observation. A major problem with the American school system is that academic success in our schools today is being reported as the result of grade inflation and the replacement of competition by "elevated self-esteem."

Indeed, many schools have rejected the idea of competition. In a phrase, the school system has eliminated motivation from the educational equation in America. Unfortunately, some students are becoming accustomed to under-performing while "coasting through school," if you will, rather than working for success.

Some students have decided school is not worth their time. They are unaware of, or are not making the connection between working hard in school and making a decent life and money after graduation.

Regarding graduation, the graduation rates of the nation's high schools reflect this reality. After hovering below the 65 percent level of students who graduated from high school in 2011, the rate actually increased to 82 percent for the academic year 2014. The question becomes, was the increase legitimate, or due to the grade inflation previously mentioned by Martin Gross? There remains more cause for concern. According to the *NY Times*, a recent evaluation of high school seniors found many are not prepared for life after graduation. The paper discovered evidence that some young people lack the skills needed for life as college students, as well as for life in the working world.

The *Times* noted that only one of ten in their study group were capable of college level reading skills. It was worse for entry-level math skills—only one in 14. According to government studies, less than 40 percent of high school seniors tested throughout the nation were capable of reading on the college level.

Following high school graduation, even fewer students graduate from colleges and universities. As the National Center for Education Statistics (NCES) reports, graduation rates for college students completing a four-year degree is only 59 percent.

Many business, academic, and military leaders are also concerned with the quality of public high school graduates coming out of our nation's school systems. The president of AT&T South Carolina, Pamela P. Lackey, made note that the graduation diplomas of today do not prepare high school graduates to enter a workforce for the today's technical jobs. The same holds true of graduates who are considering military service—many are unable to pass the entrance exams. The fact is that many high school graduates today are not able to live a sustainable, independent life alone.

What can we do? The question is, can the public school system be fixed? Why has the situation in our schools deteriorated so badly?

The bottom line is that our students are graduating without the skills they need to survive. They lack critical thinking skills, the ability to analyze, to reason logically, and they trail students of other nations in test scores, grades, skills and more.

At the same time, Hollywood and other media outlets are feeding our youth the idea that a normal life includes lots of discretionary income, big homes, and multiple cars in the garage. What they and advertisers fail to make clear to the new generation is that in order to have the cars, the house, and the money, you have to work hard.

For our youth to be successful, they must be educated. When I say educated, I am not necessarily talking about formal education, but possibly self-education. Remember the story of William Lear, you know, the guy who invented the Learjet. Not only did he create the Learjet, he is the man who gave us radios in our cars, eight-track tape players, and a host of other inventions we use every day.

He left school during the Great Depression to help his family. Lear later went back to school, but never completed his formal education. However, because he was an avid reader, he became self-educated beyond that of many who held advanced college degrees.

We live in an amazing time, a time like no other in history. We can learn anything we wish to learn on our own. The only thing needed is the motivation and drive, and the desire to succeed. More self-made millionaires than you can imagine did not attend college.

Now don't get me wrong, a college degree is necessary for certain professional careers. Medical, legal, law enforcement, aviation, military and other professions require formal, upper-level education with a four-year college degree. However, there are other positions and jobs not requiring a college diploma that pay well.

Many jobs are available throughout the nation right now. Jobs in the trades as well as service jobs. Many have done very well for themselves after training in the electrical, plumbing, and HVAC industries. Many who train in these fields go on to start their own very successful companies.

Know that the entrepreneurial spirit is alive and well in America. Be aware that those who possess that spirit must also possess critical thinking and analysis skills in order to succeed.

That is the importance of this book. For those who desire success and did not pick up everything they needed in school, this book will serve as a plan to help anyone seeking to learn on their own. This is not necessarily a textbook, but rather, a book that might spark the flame of their imagination.

If you want anyone, your child, your niece, your nephew, or other young person to be successful, give them a copy of this book. Don't tell them they have to read it; let them make their own decision.

Hopefully, they will choose wisely.

The argument for staying in school

Hey, tenth grader. So, here you are. You have made it to the "big time." Another three years and you're outta here! Right? No more high school for you, no more boring teachers, no more pansy classes, no more wasted time. Right?

Then what?

Where are you going to go? What are you going to do?

You're going to be rich, right? Live in a big house, drive a Hummer, vacation in the Rockies, snowboard Colorado in the winter and surf Hawaii the rest of the year? Sounds like a great plan. Right?

But, how are *you* going to *pay* for all of that?

I have some bad news for you, unfortunately. You are the only one who can foot that bill.

No one else wants to pay for your goodies and an extravagant lifestyle. If you really want all that "stuff," you will have to find a way to pay for it—pay for all of it. No one else wants to pay for your standard of living because, in a phrase, it is all "your stuff."

Now, here is something to think about: it is going to be very difficult to pay for all that stuff with the job you are probably going to get right out of high school. Essentially, you have the desires for a really expensive lifestyle that requires the salary of a rocket scientist. Problem is, you are not a rocket scientist. Well,—at least not yet, anyway.

This is a book every ninth or tenth grader needs to read. Some of your friends will read this book, some will not. The process of reading is very important because if you read, you will be smart. This is something you need to figure out.

If you did not read this book before the tenth grade, take heart—you can still learn a lot from this book as a junior or senior getting ready to go out in the world. In fact, some college graduates can benefit from this book. After all, that is exactly what this book is about: going out and making it in this world.

What? You say you don't want to read this book? It takes too much time? You don't like to read? You want to see the movie?

Get a grip! John Wayne (you know that old movie actor your parents admired when he was alive and probably admire even more in death) was attributed by many for saying, "Life is hard; it's harder if you're stupid." I don't know if Wayne really said it; many have said he was paraphrasing a line from the 1973 film, *The Friends of Eddie Coyle*. Regardless of where the quote originated, it is a damn fine quote.

I have to agree with Wayne's sentiment. Every day you can see the difference between people making the right decisions and those making wrong choices. Making the right decisions results in a good life while the wrong choices can create a miserable time for those who made those poor decisions.

Here are a couple of other quotes you should know and probably memorize. Bill Gates authored these two great quotes. You know who he is—one of the guys who invented all that Microsoft software and computer systems most of us use every day. He was smart, he read a lot, and he is extremely intelligent. What he said was, "Life is not fair; get used to it."

Mr. Gates is right, life is not fair. In the life on which you are about to embark with the other billions of people on this planet, you have to realize you make your own breaks. If you want to be successful, you have to be smart. If you're not smart, it stands to reason you may not be successful.

There is something else you should remember that Mr. Gates said. "Be nice to nerds. Chances are, you'll end up working for one." Those who read books become educated and intelligent, regardless of their "official" educational background. They will become the supervisors, the managers, the company owners; in short, they are the movers and shakers. Everyone else becomes . . . well, the worker bees . . . for low, or minimum wages.

The problem with many of our school systems is this: they fail to address what every young person really needs to know in order to live a rewarding and full life. Sure, you know the basics about how to live, but do you really know what it takes? What is important? What is not? What do you want to do? Where are you going to live? Will you truly be able to take care of yourself? And then there are the burning questions — how much will it cost? And how much money can you make?

If you would like to know the answers to these questions and others, and if by nature you are inquisitive, please, keep reading. If you don't care about the answers, or the concept of working, or reading is too hard for you, that's OK; you should know, however, you are not going to make as much money as you would otherwise.

Should you choose to read this book, it will be worth your time and effort in the end.

So, please, let's begin reading at the beginning, with Chapter 1.

Chapter 1 –
The schools may have failed you

PSST! Here is a secret. Don't tell anyone. If you are a graduate of the public school system, you might not be as educated as you might think. However, *you* can fix this. If you are reading this book intently, you are on the way to "fixing it." Remember, William Lear was a very successful businessman; also take note that he did not complete his formal education, having never graduated from high school. He pursued his education on his own. If you like to read and spend time analyzing what you have taken in from books, magazines, journals, films, video, and other media used to gather knowledge, you *will* learn.

Over the past few decades, many of our high school graduates have left school inadequately prepared to face life. Some of our college freshmen are entering universities without the necessary skills to succeed in school. Some college students have reading and comprehension levels lower than middle-school students. Additionally, our students lack skills in math, physics, logic, and more. Many young people fear word problems, but here's the rub—skill with word problems is a requirement for life in these modern times. If you cannot solve a word problem, you are going to have a rough go of life as you grow older.

Ask a graduating student today what they know about life and you may be surprised to find their knowledge is weak. They are unable to determine a livable budget; they have trouble balancing a checkbook; and many are incapable of figuring out how to plan meals. In short, they are unable to take care of themselves.

Life is the same as it was in past decades. Basically, you have to be smart enough to take care of yourself. Remember what John Wayne said back on page xxiv: "Life is hard; it's harder if you're stupid."

The point being is that you can choose to be stupid, or not. If you choose to be "not stupid," your parents and many wonderful teachers are willing, ready, and prepared to help you increase your knowledge so that you can be successful. They are standing by to help you acquire skills and knowledge, to become educated, to do better in the world, to really become something special. This will allow you to make your way through the marketplace of life with more rewards. You will find you will make more money than many of your classmates.

Here's something you should remember as you move through this thing called, "the rest of your life." Look around; how do some of your classmates compare with you? Keep an eye the "cool people." How do they match up to your success?

In order to do well, you have to be capable of analytical thinking and problem solving. You have to have the "smarts" to solve problems, determine the best course of action for any given situation, learn from your mistakes, and actually "do better" the next time. This is where, if you paid attention in school, you will have developed the math skills and logic to excel. Without those skills, you cannot be successful in life.

Analytical thinking is one of the most important things you can learn in school. If you are still in school, pay attention during math class. Take a logics class. Enroll in a statistics course. Study word problems until they are easy intellectual games for you. Don't watch so much TV, except the *Big Bang Theory*. If you can, watch the *Big Bang Theory*. These skills and your general knowledge will allow you to make good business decisions for your company or on your job later in life. Unfortunately, critical thinking skills, math, logic, and statistics are subjects many schools no longer teach as in the past.

If you cannot plan into the future, balance a checkbook, understand how you fit into the world, the world will pass you by. In schools, they allow everyone "to win" so that no one's feelings are hurt. What the school systems did in trying to bolster lesser performing students' self-esteem, was to overlook the most important learning for all—competition.

Make no mistake—competition is alive and well throughout the entire world. Unfortunately, many school systems have sliced the competitive spirit out of the hearts of most students. Learning to be competitive is one of life's most important lessons.

Pay attention. What follows is really important.

Competition in the business world is very real. It is also present in the military, med school, law school, at McDonald's, Wal-Mart, and the local 7-11 store, or wherever else you might find your first job. Competition allows the cream to rise to the top of the milk; another way to view this is that those with talent and potential will not be satisfied to continue working menial jobs at a minimum wage for very long. They will continue on to professional education or start their own businesses. They will become millionaires while their peers, who were only interested in having fun and causing trouble in school, will continue working jobs at lower levels while protesting for higher pay.

Read the previous paragraph again. Slowly. Take it all in. Pay very close attention. Make certain you fully understand the intent of the message. It is important!

Over the last three or four decades, the school systems in all 50 states have moved toward this "no competition—everyone wins" teaching style.

Well, there will always be winners, and losers. This will never change. The school systems have decided they wanted to make things "fair." They started awarding participation prizes to keep children from "feeling bad" because they lost or failed in their project, or their sports competition, or their musical recital. Consequently, they also stopped teaching one of the most important lessons every child needs to learn: losing or failing is a part of the equation for success, how to analyze what caused the failure, what to do to prevent it in the future — and *how to become successful.*

This is a very important lesson every kid needs to know.

For the price of feeling bad or losing once in a while, the lesson students learn is priceless. This is one area in which private schools and home schooling are seeing success.

In much of the literature about the differences between public schools, private schooling, and home schooling, the quality of private and home schooling has outpaced the public market. In performance and knowledge tests, public school students lag behind the private sector. This is according to research by Michael Cogan, the director of research and analysis at the University of St. Thomas.

What Cogan discovered and reported was that home schooled students had higher entrance scores than other freshmen college students. They had also completed more college level work than others before graduating high school. The average grade point average (GPA) for home schooled students in their freshman year of college was 3.37, compared to 3.08 for other freshmen. And here is a really important statistic—66.7 percent of home schooled students successfully graduated from college, compared to non-home schooled students, who only attained a rate of 57.5 percent.

Here is the odd thing about the perception of home schooled students: When talking about the home schooled graduates, non-home schooled students will say home schooled children are "weird," "they don't fit in," "they will not be successful," and "they are unable to participate in sports."

Whenever I hear someone say something like this, I look that person square in the eye and simply say, "Tim Tebow."

Tebow is only one of many of the famous who were home schooled. Others on the list include presidents, authors, artists, composers, judges, and more. Some of the celebrities on the list with Tebow are the musicians Taylor Swift, Justin Timberlake, Justin Bieber, and Louis Armstrong. Actors who were home school include Alan Alda, Christina Aguilera, Dakota Fanning, and Jennifer Love Hewitt. The list of home schooled inventors contain Alexander Graham Bell, Eli Whitney, Thomas Edison, as well as the Wright Brothers. Famous authors taught at home include C.S. Lewis, Alex Haley, Mark Twain, Pearl S. Buck, Robert Frost, and Agatha Christie.

Many from the public school group are trying to justify their choices to the rest of the world.

Now, don't get me wrong. I am a graduate of the public school system, but it was from a another time. Things were different then—we played kickball, dodgeball, and we *competed*. Not everyone was a winner. We studied history, math, science, English, Civics, and more. We had wonderful teachers who taught classes and helped us learn. It was a time when both administrators and parents backed up the teachers in teacher-student confrontations. And if we did not do our homework, or we got in trouble at school, many of us found ourselves in more trouble at home when our parents found out about our school trouble.

Oh yes, and when I found myself lacking in certain areas of education, I grabbed a book and self-studied until I got what I needed. Just like Mr. Lear...

Again, I come to the point that it is *your* choice. You can choose to be ignorant, educated, smart, or dumb. If you choose wisely, you are going to make money, maybe even a lot of money, but more importantly, you will enjoy your life. Choose wrong, however, and life will be hard, just as Mr. Wayne said.

Good luck on your choices.

Chapter 2 – Self-assessment

Go on. Do it!
　　Look into the mirror!
　　What do you see?

This is where you first begin. Take a good look at the person looking back at you from the mirror.

How do you like that person? Who is he or she? Where is that person going? What will that person become? Is that person going to finish school? Will that person go to college? What kind of a job will that person do? Might that person go into the military? Is that person a good person?

That person is you.

So, you, what kind of a human being are you? Who do you want to be? Who might you become?

Right now, you are at the beginning of your life. You have choices. You can choose who you want to be, where you want to live, what you want to do in your working life, how much money you want to make, or how little. There are so many other choices available to you.

Let's start with the first, most basic, question. Are you a good person?

Because you are reading this book, you probably have ambition. After all, you're thinking about it. And you do have the choice — either to be good or ... not so good. That is your first choice and there is something you need to understand about that first choice.

By choosing to be good, the world opens up to you. If you choose otherwise, the world will lock you out.

When the world opens up to you, it will present you with many more choices. You can choose from anything you wish. The job you want, where you want to live, whether or not to marry, how many children to have, and the people with whom you would like to associate.

Understand that choosing to be good is hard work and in some cases, a degree of luck. It begins with the people with whom you choose "to hang." Good friends are hard to come by and they will be a reflection of your soul. If you choose friends who are good, this goodness will feed on itself and become much more. It will follow you wherever you go. People around you and your friends will recognize the goodness of your group and they will work very hard to help you and your friends succeed.

However, if you choose unwisely and associate with people who are not so good, you and your friends will probably get in trouble. The degree of trouble will influence the rest of your life. Essentially, if you want to go into medicine, the military, work in government, go into law enforcement, become an airline pilot, or do any number of other jobs requiring a clean background, you must keep your record spotless.

If your friends think a good time involves alcohol or weed and you are with them when they are arrested, your chances of enjoying a professional career, or going to the college of your choice, may be completely dashed.

Always remember the choices you make now will influence the rest of your life. To achieve your dreams, you have to work hard for those dreams and you have to keep "your nose clean."

A few young people get into trouble without realizing it by the way they drive. Careless and reckless operation of a motor vehicle can ruin a life faster than anyone may realize. Another way to get into trouble is by drinking underage, especially while driving.

Many teenagers fail to understand that traffic violations, accidents, or a DUI can ruin a life. The problem with a car accident is that once it happens, there is no going back. If you cause bodily harm or death by way of your careless or negligent operation of a car, there is a very good chance you will go to jail, pay extremely high fines, and never be in a position to drive ever again.

Seems pretty unfair, doesn't it? A number of people will say, "No, not really." You would be one of them if someone you loved was killed or injured.

If you are at fault for operating a car dangerously and you kill or hurt someone, the punishment should fit the crime. And that's what it is, a crime.

People caught in this situation usually whine, "We were just having fun!"

You have to realize that driving is something you must approach very seriously. There are a lot of things you can do to have fun, but when driving a car or truck, focus on what you are doing.

Assuming your driving record is good, let's take a look at what you might want to do after high school. You have so many options compared to the generations before you. And just as your parents and their parents had to do when they were your age, you must determine exactly what it is *you* want to do.

Once out of high school, graduates usually go one of three different directions. One option is college or further training. Another is the military. Or you might decide to get a job.

There are, however, more ways to make money than you were taught in school. Hopefully, this little book will give you some good ideas on how to make a living and as well as make a life. It will also let you in on few secrets about how much it will cost.

Chapter 3 – Choices

You need to understand that life, this thing you are about to enter all on your own, is full of choices. As you start out on your journey, you must make many decisions and choices. The decisions you make are going to either create a wonderful experience for you, or not. It is, in a short phrase, *your choice*.

Right now, you have the choice to be good or not so good. You can do the right thing, or not. It is really that simple. Be good, or misbehave. It all boils down to the choices you make. And it starts with the first choice, to be good, or cause trouble.

If you make good choices, your life will be filled with wonderful things—friends, jobs, money, prestige, and more. Goodness will lead to more goodness and you will really have a great time living your life. Life will seem too short, because it is true about life—it really is too short. It will be rewarding and you will enjoy yourself immensely.

On the other hand, if you make bad choices, well, life will be a load. You will not enjoy yourself and it could turn out to be very long, especially if you are sitting somewhere you would prefer not to be sitting—such as in jail. The ugly thing about ending up in jail is that you can get there completely by accident.

Again, we go back to this idea of choices. One of the first things you will discover is that you have to choose your friends. You must choose your friends very carefully. If you choose good people as your friends, you and your friends will interact synergistically (that's a big word to say "work together") positively for the common good. Consequently, you and your companions will create more good right out of thin air. It is an amazing process.

If you choose poor friends, they may be the sort of people who will get you in trouble; they might be into drugs, drinking, or any number of other unlawful acts. You might find yourself arrested merely because you were hanging out with these "friends" at the wrong time.

Here's the important thing to realize and know about about "friends" like these—if you are arrested with them, it will shut more than half of the doors to your future.

There are many positions and jobs you cannot hold if you have a police record. I know it sounds harsh, but you have to look at it the way the public sees it. For instance, take airline pilots. Do you think people have to trust an airline pilot? After all, they are going to have hundreds of lives in their hands. The airline company must be able to trust every pilot they hire to fly their airplanes. If they don't have a warm and fuzzy feeling about hiring someone as a pilot, the company will not offer that person a job.

One metric a company uses to determine if they can trust a pilot to fly their aircraft safely and appropriately is their driving record. Anyone applying for a job to fly hundreds of people around in a multimillion dollar jet probably cannot be trusted if they have a record of constantly breaking traffic laws. Those who choose to speed or drive carelessly will probably not follow the aviation regulations regarding the operation of aircraft. Again, it all comes back to the idea of choices. You can choose to follow the law, or break it.

Going back to the choice of your friends, choose good people as your friends. If you do, you will probably do good throughout your life. Choosing the wrong friends, however, may take you down a path from which you may not be able to recover.

Read the end of the last paragraph again.

Slowly.

Understand it.

I have known families in which one child chose well, another badly. The child that chose well did great things, kept good people close as friends, enjoyed wonderful rewards and great achievements. Toward their later years, one was financially secure, lived comfortably, and continued to thrive. Their sibling, however, well, not so much.

Here is something important to remember—and this is very important—if you make the wrong choice, as I mentioned before, there are no "do-overs." You won't have a second chance. Once you are criminally convicted, there are things you will not be able to do.

Take a look at any newspaper or online publication. They are filled with stories of young people who made the wrong decisions. Some of the stories are heartbreaking and you have to wonder, "What were they thinking?"

Life after making a wrong choice can become depressing. In fact, some bad choices may actually end your life.

If you are projecting an image that threatens others and you scare people to the point they literally fear for their lives, they might feel a need to protect themselves and may very well do so.

There are too many stories in social media and the newspapers and radio about individuals dying because of bad behavior. It does not have to involve threatening behavior either—sometimes a young person will make a decision to do something they think is "fun" and accidentally ends up dead.

There are numerous incidents where someone thought, "it would be cool," to say... jump off the roof of a house into a pool. Worked well when just jumping in. Then someone else has the great idea of doing a flip off the roof. In the process, they miss the pool and hit their head on the concrete below.

In such cases, witnesses stand around clucking their tongues and shaking their heads. They are the same people who, only moments before, were encouraging the bad behavior.

It does one well to remember that oft repeated phrase my mother passed my way more than a couple of times: "If all your friends are going to jump off a cliff, are you going to, also?"

Just because everyone is doing it, whatever *it* is, doesn't make it right.

Chapter 4 – The cool apartment
(pad, crib, or place)

One topic many schools may fail to teach is the idea of how much it will cost to live, after leaving home. Unfortunately, many parents also fail to teach their children this important life lesson. Consequently, a number of high school graduates enter life poorly prepared to succeed. They have little clue as to how to make money, how much money they need, or how much their monthly bills will total.

Now the question is: Do you want to be one of the successful? Or, will you be happy being less than successful? Do you really have an idea of how much it will cost to live? More importantly, do you know how much money you must make in order to pay your bills?

First, let's look at how much it will cost you to live by yourself after high school. Here is a list of basics along with their approximate costs as of 2016.

Food, this is the first priority. For guys, base price for food is $223 on the low side, $448 on the high side, with a national average of $364 a month. The numbers for girls run $198, $395, and $310 a month, respectively.

Average rent around the nation is about $1050 per month for a basic one-bedroom apartment. If you live in the middle of America, you might find something for about $600 or so. If you want to live in San Diego, New York, Chicago, or Miami, average rent for a one bedroom in these cities can reach as high as $3000 or $4000 per month. The national monthly average for electricity in the northeast is $111, in the south $120, and in the mountainous central region, $85. For the US, the monthly average works out to $104. For telephones, most will opt for a cell phone with no land line. More than likely, the land line will be cheaper, but in this time of constant contact, it does make sense to have only a cell. The average cost of a cell phone depends on the plan and the model of phone you purchase. Plan on costs running somewhere between $50 and $125 per month, or more.

One costly item for all of us is transportation. The US Department of Transportation reports that Americans spend nine percent of their income in "location efficient environments" and 25 percent in "auto dependent exurbs." The average American family spends 25 percent of their income on transportation.

Rent (one-bedroom apt)	$1050
Electricity	$100
Telephone (basic land line)	$55
Food (eating cheap)	$230
Transportation	$350
Total	$1785

Table 1. Basic survival budget.

What it boils down to is this: During the first year you are out on your own, you need to have $21,420 just to pay your bills. In order to do that, you have to make approximately $25,000. Remember, even though it is "your" money, you have to pay taxes on it. The first year you are on your own, you will have to pay $1000 to $2600 in taxes; so, if you are working for $12 an hour ($4.35 more than the present minimum wage of $7.65) you will make about $24,000 for the year. Take out $2000 for your tax bill and that will leave you about $22,000—just barely enough to make your basic living expenses.

Oh, wait a minute! Guess what? That's still not enough!

There are other things you must pay for. The first, and most important, is you. You must create a savings account and the first check you should write each month is into that account. You must save money to get ahead in this world. At a minimum, you should place $100 a month into *your* savings. It is very important!

What does that mean? Well, you simply have to make more money. You must make another $1200 to fund the account, but wait! You have to bring in even more money to pay the taxes on that extra money.

Bottom line—you must make $26,200 by the end of the year just to get by and fund $1200 in savings. That means your gross paycheck should be $31,000 for the year, or $2583 monthly, or $596 per week.

Can you make that much? Is it possible? Remember, this assumes your employer pays the cost of your health insurance and you are living in a tax friendly state. You may have additional deductions from your paycheck for state tax and insurance, or other considerations.

So what does all this really mean?

If you need $21,420 to satisfy your bills the first year you are on your own, you need to make certain you make at least $25,000. Making $25,000 a year is a pretty tall order for someone just out of high school with no real, or very little, work experience. "But I have experience," you say. "I worked at the local hamburger citadel cooking fries and making 'burgers."

How much money did you make working at a quick food joint on weekends and after school? Minimum wage? What? Maybe $8 or $9 an hour part-time?

You need $25,000 and to make that much money working full time requires a complete understanding of the following formula.

$25,000 divided by 52 weeks
divided by 40 hours/week

Mathematically, this equates to minimum hourly wage of $25,000 / 2080 = $12.02 per hour.

So there you have it. You must work all day for $12.02 an hour — just to pay your bills and fund your savings account. Remember — this only pays your bills and leaves nothing left over for things like movies, parties, gifts, or weekend trips with your friends. And what about those other things you would like to buy, things like cell phones, X-Boxes, or computers?

If you want to buy any of those big-ticket items, or more importantly, a car, you have to plan carefully. You can take out credit to buy some of them, but you have to be very careful (see Chapter 10).

In order to purchase expensive things like a car, you have to plan how to pay the bills those items will create. Indeed, when it comes to buying a car, remember you must consider the other expenses associated with auto ownership (see Chapter 8).

The way to determine if you can afford the big-ticket items is to throw them into a variant of the equations above. In other words...,

Total annual living expenses	$21,420
Savings	$1,200
Electronic devices	$3,000
Movies and other entertainment	$2,000
New total	$27,620

Table 2. What it's really going to cost.

To bring home $27,620 to pay for your living expenses, savings, electronic devices, and other entertainment, the tax bill will be about $4800. This means you must make about $32,500 just to break even. The hourly wage required is:

$$\$32,500 / 2080 = \$15.63 \text{ per hour}$$

As you can see from the math, making the money you need to survive will be no easy task. One thing making it more difficult is the number of people applying for the available jobs, particularly in a tight economy. In many cases, there are more applicants trying to get a job than there are jobs. This means employers can pick and choose who they will hire. While you may hold out for higher pay, the next three people in line behind you may opt to work for less, being happy just to have a job.

This leaves you with few options. Right away, take the first job you are offered, it will put money in your pocket now. Keep looking for a better job while you are doing the best job possible for your new boss. You should always be looking for the next better job, you just don't have to advertise it. (See Chapter 7.)

What makes you so different from all the others in your graduating class? How do you stand out? What will you do differently from your peers that will allow a potential employer to make more money by hiring you over someone else?

News flash: No one owes you a better paying job. Just like everything in life, you are going to get what you deserve.

Here is another hard unpleasant fact—it takes a lot of hard work to get what you want out of life. Oh yes, if you want the big house, the Hummer, and the vacations on the snow in Colorado, you have to make the money to pay for it. The question now becomes, how are you going to make that much money?

Making that kind of money is tough. Over the last couple of decades, the media has not made it any easier for you. Whenever you turn on a television or go to a movie, Hollywood has fed you a constant diet of "the easy life." If you believe what you see on TV, everyone lives in big houses and drives brand new cars. And not just any big house or any car—they are the very best houses and the coolest cars.

Unfortunately, with the media feeding us a constant barrage of costly lifestyles as normal, reinforced by advertising encouraging Americans to buy the most expensive goods and services now rather than later, it is no wonder the nation is in a financial meltdown. This creates young people's expectations that they are entitled to all the wonderful things they see on the big and small screens. There is also a monumental disconnect in their minds between the houses and extravagant cars — and the respective price tags.

To put this into better perspective for many, a large house requires $30,000 a year or more to maintain. Throw in another $1000 to $5000 for utilities. Food for two can easily exceed another $9000 or $10,000. Luxury cars will add another $10,000 to the annual budget. Entertainment and other "goodies" will require about $12,000. The lifestyle you see on television will easily cost more than $75,000. In order to pay $75,000 for your lifestyle, your gross annual salary has to match or exceed $95,000. Or, an hourly pay rate of $45.68.

That is a lot of money.

It also begs the question of what can you do that might be worth $45 an hour or more? Is there a company out there willing to pay you that much?

OK, get ready, brace yourself and gird your loins!

As only a high school graduate, there is little chance you can do anything to make $45 an hour. Life is not fair. People like your mom and dad have been working a long time and they have figured out one of two things. Either you make a lot of money, or you live within your means.

What living within your means is all about is just that. You cannot have more bills than you have paycheck. If you are bringing in $2000 a month, your bills cannot total more than $2000.

This includes all your bills—food, rent, utilities, transportation; and the first thing on that list you should pay before all others is you. You should be putting 10 percent of your paycheck into savings. (Please see Chapter 9 for more detailed information on the importance of saving.)

Without more schooling or specialized training or working for yourself, there is little chance you are going to make more than $18,000 a year. To make more money, you must discover a way of making money unique to you.

For instance, going to college and specializing in a field that shows great growth potential might work. Going into the military and obtaining specialized training to allow you to make more money later on the civilian job market may be an option. You may be one of those who would excel in a specialized trade school. There is also a possibility that—if you are observant enough—you can figure out a special niche in which you can build your own business. Later chapters will cover some of these ideas.

The bottom line is this—it takes a lot more money to live than you can imagine. Living with a roommate may help financially, but only to a limited degree. Here is something else to remember; at some point in your future, you will be thinking of starting your own family. Regardless of whether you are a female or male, you should be preparing for that part of your future.

It is very expensive to live on your own. It will be even more expensive when you are talking about raising *children*. And yes, that time is a long way away off if you are reading this as a tenth grader. It is pretty close if you have just graduated from college. Regardless, you will be surprised by how quickly that time will be upon you. *Now is the time* to prepare for those decisions coming later in your life.

You can get married, have children, and try to make a living while going to school all at the same time. This can be a recipe for disaster; however, some couples manage. If you want to avoid the disaster, you need to know how to plan.

If you plan properly, you can arrange it so that you can go through college, the military, a trade school, or start your own business, and then have the money to bring your children into this world, while you can still enjoy your life.

Your ability to enjoy your life starts right now. Again, you have choices to make.

Sure, right now, you just want to go out and have fun and you can do that immediately. However, remember the choices you make today will influence all aspects of your future life.

To avoid misery, take the proper course of action now. Is it the "cool" thing to do? Maybe. Maybe not. Remember this—later when you are standing on solid financial ground and you have a happy family, a good house in a safe neighborhood, and driving a comfortable car, some of the "cool" people today will be very envious of your position later.

They will also realize they were once in the very same position to make all of the right decisions as you. Only now, they are too far down the road of life and the poor decisions they made earlier may have cost them harshly, both in money and relationships.

If you are going to succeed and be happy, just know it will take hard work and sacrifice early in your life—to enjoy the best years of your life.

It is a choice, a choice that is yours alone to choose. Your parents don't have a say in your choices. Sure, they have an influence and you should listen to what they say. After all, they have already been through what you are experiencing now and they have already made their choices. Listen to them, observe them, and analyze what they did right, what they did wrong. Use them and their friends as role models. Repeat everything they did right, avoid all they did wrong.

Make the right choices for yourself.

Chapter 5 –
Your grocery bill and clothes

Once you are actually out on your own, you will find life might be different from what you expected. For instance, when you go to the 'fridge to get something to eat, you will discover you can only do that if *you* went to the store, decided what to buy, paid for it, brought it home, and put it in the 'fridge for later. This was something your parents probably did for you in the past.

Another thing you may find disturbing comes at the end of a meal in a restaurant. You have to pay the bill. Again, your parents probably paid your tab. Well, rest assured this responsibility now squarely falls on you. Now that you are on your own, you have to make certain you have enough money to pay your bills. This includes your cost of eating.

Have you given any thought to how much food will cost? (See the chapters 4 and 6.) As with anything in life, planning and arranging your food takes time and energy. When it comes to food, you have two options. One is to go to the grocery store and stock up on various supplies you can prepare in your own kitchen. The other is to go out. Most of us do a combination of these two options, based on the amount of money we make and the level of our "discretionary income."

The trick to your grocery bill is to budget enough money in order to eat properly.

So, how much does it cost to eat? As mentioned in the last chapter, it depends on whether you are a girl or guy and if you eat light or heavy. As noted, it will be about $285 for girls and about $325 for guys each month. Of course, the more you eat out, the more you'll pay for your monthly food bill.

First, eating properly does not mean going to a fast food restaurant and eating your fill of burgers, fries, and sodas. Certainly, you can do that, but doing so is not healthy. In fact, it can be dangerous. I remember my cousin, who is a doctor, telling her father the story of an 18-year-old student she examined in the emergency room. Once he was away from his parents, he began eating as he pleased. He liked burgers and fries — a lot — which is exactly what he ate for three months. Without the nourishment of "live" nutrients found in vegetables and fruits, this young man developed a medical problem known as rickets. The common cause of which is a deficiency of vitamin D or calcium in the diet.

You can live on burgers and fries for about $13 a day. However as just noted, it will probably make you sick. For less than that, you can go to the grocery store and buy healthy foods. The trade-off is that you must prepare the food at home. This takes time, which is the reason for the success of the fast food industry.

You can frequent other restaurants for a healthy meal. However, a meal in a reputable restaurant serving good salads and vegetables with the main course will be more expensive than burgers and fries. A decent meal in a good restaurant typically runs between $12 to $24, possibly more.

The trick to eating well, and properly, without becoming bored out of your mind, is to balance the number times you eat at good restaurants, fast food joints, and at home. The ratio of going out to eat compared to eating in depends upon how much money you make. Remember, if you make more money, you have more of that "discretionary income" mentioned earlier. This will allow you to go out more often.

One thing to be aware of and something you should avoid is using your credit card to pay for restaurant meals. (See Chapter 10 for information on how to do this, if you decide to pay by card.) Many of your friends will go out every Friday and Saturday for dinner and movies. They will ask you to come along and you will want to. Here's the question: Can you afford it?

Some of your friends actually will be able to pay for that kind of lifestyle. Some of your other friends will be burning up their credit cards to keep up with them. Don't be tempted to follow their lead. Be content with eating at home more often and going out only when you can afford it. One benefit of doing this is that when you do go out, you will appreciate the treat even more.

Another area in which you must have money is for buying clothes. This might be more of a girl problem than a guy problem. Guys will wear a pair of underwear until there is no longer a resemblance to underwear. They will also wear a pair of jeans for a month without washing them.

Girls on the other hand, tend to buy clothes more often than guys. Many young women have found themselves overspending and in trouble in short order. Girls, don't fall into this trap. Remember, there are some who can afford to "shop 'til they drop," and there are those who must be very careful with their money. This goes for guys, too. There are some young men who are real shoppers while more young women are becoming frugal. For both sexes—be careful.

While guys can wear jeans for the longest time, in the working world, they may have to wear "business clothes." Consequently, both young men and women entering the work force should budget a certain amount of their income to replenish their clothing. Again, don't go crazy; spend what you can afford. Also remember that fancy clothes might need to be *dry cleaned*. This could amount to quite a bit more in cash outlay—and you have to pay for it. You should always look as professional as possible on any job.

Chapter 6 – Your budget

So, how much do you think it will *really cost* to live? Have you given thought to how much your parents have been paying on your behalf for your past existence on the planet? In Chapter 4, I touched only on the basics. Now, let's throw in some real numbers.

Most recent high school graduates have little knowledge and less experience regarding finances and budget planning. Consequently, when they get out on their own, most are shocked by how much money it takes just to live.

Here is a list of the things you should consider in developing your budget:

Food – no matter what, you have to eat
Housing – got to have a place to sleep
Electricity – got to have the buzz
Savings – should be paid first

Telephone – must be able to talk
Water – the magical fluid of life
Garbage – someone has to take out the trash
Sewerage – sometimes included with water bill
Other bills – stuff like credit cards
Car payment – could be big or small, even $0
Car insurance – this will be huge
Gas – this can also be big
Car maintenance – depends on car's age
Clothing – more for girls, less for boys
Dining out – everyone needs to go out occasionally
Entertainment – goes along with dining out

Now that you know a little about what you will spend your money on, let's throw some realistic numbers in the plan and see what the real bottom line might be.

Food	$300
Housing	$800
Electricity	$125
Savings	$150
Telephone	$90
Water	$50
Garbage	$30
Sewerage	$15
Other bills	$150
Car payment	$225
Car insurance	$300
Gas	$200
Maintenance	$40
Clothing	$100
Dining out	$50
Entertainment	$50
Total	$2675

Table 3. A more realistic monthly budget.

The total of $2,675 amounts to more than $32,100 for the year. Any which way you cut it, life expenses are costly. Especially if you want to live a lifestyle including anything more than the basics. (Notice that I bumped up the savings on this budget.)

Oh yes, don't forget you have to make enough money to pay the taxes on the $32,100 cost of living. This will be about $3600. So, just to get by, you are looking at a minimum income of $35,700, or almost $3000 per month.

To make this much money on an hourly job, your rate has to be $17.16 per hour. That is without overtime. This is to say that if you go in on a Monday through Friday job and you punch the clock for a 40-hour workweek, the equation will look like this:

$$40 \text{ hours} \times 52 \text{ weeks} =$$
$$2{,}080 \text{ hours} \times \$17.16 = \$35{,}700.$$

This will equal $2975 per month, or $687 per week, or ($32,100/365=) $97.81 per day, each day of the year.

That's a lot of money. And yet, it is not.

The questions you need to ask are: Can you make that much money? Can you command that level of a salary? What about raises later?

If you cannot make $36k a year, the next question you need to ask is how can you make up the difference? What other options do you have for making money?

Here's one: How about buying a house? And then acquiring enough roommates to cover the cost of the mortgage. And maybe the utilities.

For example, if you were to acquire a modest three-bedroom house with a mortgage of about $1000 a month with utilities averaging $200, your total cash required would be $1200 each month. With two roommates paying $600 a month for the rent of one bedroom and $50 a month for electricity, your income would be $1300 a month.

After you pay the mortgage and utilities, you will be $100 to the good for the month. Another way look at this is to realize you are making $1200 a year while saving $10,800 a year for not paying rent on a one-bedroom apartment and the associated utilities.

You have to do your research on this idea, however. Some localities have either city ordinances or HOA rules about more than two non-related people living in the same house. Again, do your homework.

Could you imagine living rent-free for three years? By saving $1000 a month for rent and utilities, a very smart and enterprising young person could bank more than $36,000 during those three years.

If you were to invest wisely, there would be no telling how much interest it could earn over those three years. If you are disciplined and deposited $1000 a month into an account each month for three years, at possibly 2.5 percent, the deposits will grow to a total of $37,400. Invested wisely in the market, you may be able to see a return perhaps as high as 17 percent in riskier options. The total might grow to perhaps $46,000 or more. (See Chapter 9.)

Chapter 7 – Now that you have a budget, you need a job

What did you want to become when you were a kid? Most of us wanted to grow up to be firefighters, police officers, astronauts, or teachers. Everyone must do something to make money in order to keep a roof over their head, put food on the table, and pay bills. The question becomes, just what do *you* want *to do* to make *your* money.

The first thing to realize is that in order to make money doing something you really enjoy will take careful planning, regardless of your educational plans and the school from which you graduate. It could be high school, college, or grad school.

Always remember this important concept: *If you really enjoy what you do for a living, you will never work a day in your life.*

Here is another important concept: Sometimes you might have to work a job you might not enjoy—for a while—in order to get where you want to go. Another way to look at this might be to view your current job as a stepping-stone for the next, better job. This is why it is important to always do your best in any job you are working, regardless of how well you like or dislike the job. Regardless, remember this—*always* do your best while working for someone else—and even more so if you are working for yourself. Keep stretching as much as you can.

By doing so, you will be successful at whatever you do. Additionally, you will have a great time at work. And here is another important reason for doing a great job—past employers will really go to bat for you when you apply for your next job.

Each job following your first job should be better than the last. Another way to view this progression is like this: If you want to be an astronaut and your first flying job is flying little airplanes, your second job should put you in medium-sized airplanes. The next job should put you into a bigger airplane, maybe even a jet.

The real trick to flying jets is to figure out that is what you really want to do—earlier in your life rather than later. The earlier you can determine your career goals, the better. Some are lucky, having been born knowing exactly what they would do from an early age. Others, not so lucky.

If you fall into the latter category, don't despair. Here's what you need to realize: Your first few jobs can be used to "try out" different fields as a way to find *the* job that really excites you. Just be careful not to allow working different jobs to become a lifestyle.

For some high school graduates, working various jobs in different industries did become their preferred lifestyle. The danger with this is never settling down and establishing roots in a particular field. You must "establish" yourself to create a creditable job history with a record of a decent income. If you are jumping from one job to another early in your working life, it is safe to say your salary will stay somewhere near starting levels as you move from job to job. Jumping jobs works to increase your salary only if you are already established in your field and then, only if you play by certain rules.

In the "old days," everyone understood that after graduating from high school or college, you would go get a great job with a wonderful company. You would work hard for your company over the next 40 or 50 years, after which, the company would reward you for your hard work by giving you merit pay raises and annual cost of living adjustments to keep up with inflation. You could also look forward to a decent retirement with health benefits for the rest of your life.

Not anymore. Those old rules no longer apply. For you who intend to graduate from college, along with those who already hold college degrees, you must realize that in order to boost your salary by any significance, you will have to play the job-jumping game. This is the game in which you seek a job in your field with another company that is willing to pay you significantly more for the same job you are doing with your current company. This allows you room to negotiate a higher, more appropriate salary with your current company. Or, move on to the new company, which is willing to give you more money for your efforts.

It is what it is—jumping from one job to another is all—*a game*. For those of you recently graduated, you need to remember that as you start on your way to living the rest of your lives, there are rules. Some rules you need to follow, others not so much.

The important thing about the rules is knowing which you must follow and which you can break without consequence. Another way of looking at it is this: Some rules are law or regulation and others are recommendations or good practices. One you can break, the other, the regulations and rules, you cannot.

Chapter 8 – Got to have wheels

OK, you are out living on your own, or maybe with a roommate. Either way, you have to be able to "get around." So, you have to have transportation.

This is where the "city kids" have a distinct advantage. In large, metropolitan areas, public transportation tends to be refined. There are buses, taxi cabs, subways, and other modes of public transportation. One aspect of getting around lately is Uber, available almost anywhere. If you don't have access to other types of transportation, you might have to buy a car.

Do you know how much a car will cost in these modern times? Many high school students drive cars, and maybe even completed a drivers' education course. However, most teenagers do not know how much a car will cost or what it takes to maintain one over time.

When it comes to cars, most of us want something jazzy, flashy, or "really cool." Problem is, the more jazz, flash, and coolness you desire, the more expensive the car. Remember, cars really are *very* expensive. If you are one of the fortunate few who have parents who can help you with the purchase of your first car, eventually you will have to replace that car. Again, it is still going to be extremely expensive.

Go back and review Chapter 6 regarding keeping transportation within your budget. In the following two chapters, you can see what it will take to make the money to buy a car and how to save for the either the down payment or the full price of your car.

Our love affair with cars began near the turn of the last century. No, not 2000, but rather 1900. Although your grandparents and great-grandparents struggled through The Great Depression of the 1930s, many began acquiring their first cars. Cars and pickup trucks became an important part of American life because of the makeup of our land. Cars became a necessity rather than a luxury, especially in rural America. Unlike Europe, where communities are closer to one another, America was spread out with great expanses of fields and forests between small towns and cities.

If you are considering your first car, the first thing you need to think about are the pros and cons of buying new. The advantage of buying a new car is that they tend to be more "maintenance free." The attraction of used cars is that they cost less, but may require more shop time. You have to take a look at the entire cost of ownership from purchase to maintenance. Many older and well-established adults actually refuse to buy a new car because a new car loses so much value after you take delivery and drive it off the lot.

When you drive a new car away from the dealer, it loses about 20 percent of its value immediately. Depreciation can reach as high as 50 percent within two-and-a-half years of buying a new car. Realize that you are paying an awful lot of money for the privilege of saying, "I bought a new car."

Many of your friends will think your car is really cool and you will bask in the glow for a little while. Others will think you really don't know how to handle your money. After a while, you may even find yourself wishing you had bought a more reasonable car — especially after the reality of writing a check for the monthly payment kicks in.

Buying a car is serious business that requires a lot of investigation and decision-making. You can't go out and buy a car "just because you really like it." Unfortunately, for many, that's exactly what they do. They may buy a car based on emotion rather than good, solid research.

Take a look of the question of mileage. A car with a big engine that gets only 15 miles to the gallon will cost twice as much for gas as a smaller car with a rating of 30 mpg.

To illustrate, assume you drive 17,500 miles a year. This equates to just less than 1,500 miles a month. Now, let's take two different vehicles. The first will be the Ford F150 pickup and the second, a Toyota Corolla. At the start of 2016, the price for a new F150 listed at about $29,800. The EPA rating for mileage on the F150 is 18 mpg in the city and 25 mpg on the highway with a combined average of 20 mpg.

A new Toyota Corolla costs about $17,500. The EPA mileage estimate is 29 mpg in the city and 38 mpg on the highway. Using the same city to highway ratio as for the F150 above, mileage is approximately 32 mpg for the Corolla.

OK, hold on to your socks because now we're getting down to the nitty-gritty.

With today's current gas prices averaging about $2 per gallon, the F150 will cost $1750 for the year, or about $145 a month. The Corolla's fuel bill will only be $1094 annually or $91 each month. That is a big difference.

In the coming years, there is a possibility gas will again rise to $4 a gallon—or more. For the owner of a Ford F150, this means almost $300 monthly, just for gas to drive the big Ford. For the same distance in the Corolla, the price would be $182. Of course, with the higher the cost of gasoline, the larger the spread of operating costs become between the two types of vehicles.

Paying extra money for gas seems like a huge waste of money. In fact, that's exactly how many see it. Of course, if you have money to burn or it really is growing off trees, it doesn't matter. However, check the next chapter to see what you could do with all the money you might save by driving a smaller car.

In addition to spending money on gas, there are other things that will cost money to keep your car running. The first of these include oil changes.

Every three to four thousand miles, you must make sure to change your oil. This will cost $20 to $100, depending on the make and model of your car and where you have the work done. This amounts to an additional cost of $80 to as much as $600 a year or more, depending on how much you drive. If you do not drive a lot, you should change your oil quarterly. This means a minimum of four oil changes each year.

Make sure you do change your oil at least that often. It is much cheaper to change the oil than to repair or replace the engine. Paying $80 to $600 a year for oil changes beats a $4000 engine replacement anytime.

Oil changes are only a part of the expense of auto ownership. There are other maintenance expenses you must be aware of and willing to pay. One cost you cannot afford to overlook includes the tires and brakes.

If you are out driving on worn tires or your brakes are so thin they cannot stop your car safely and you have an accident, the police will probably charge you. If charged, you may become liable for damages caused by your negligence. And yes, that is how it will probably be viewed—as negligence. This is why it is very important to carry liability insurance.

Car insurance is not cheap, but you must have it. You cannot afford to be caught driving without liability coverage. If you cause an accident and you do not have liability insurance, those you injure may sue you to the point you may never be able to recover financially. Even with liability insurance, there remains a possibility of having to pay a large sum of money because of the accident.

To explain, let's say you have a liability policy on your car for $500,000. Following an accident which you caused, regardless of being charged or not, you could face a civil lawsuit. If there were three other families involved and each decides to sue you for the accident, their lawyers may successfully argue you should pay each family $400,000. This amounts to a $1.2 million judgment against you.

Your insurance company will pay the limits of your insurance policy, provided you were not involved in any illicit activity during the accident. This will leave you about $700,000 short on paying the entire sum. In the worst case that could or might happen, you may be held responsible for paying the $700,000.

And you say, "I don't have $700,000."

That does not matter. They'll take it out of your paycheck. The court has the option of taking it out of your paycheck—all of your future paychecks—until the $700,000 debt is paid. This is called wage garnishment and the court may take part of your paycheck until the debt is paid.

The court will determine exactly what you need to survive. And we're talking about bare bones survival. Everything else you bring home on your paycheck will go into an account set up to pay back the remaining $700,000. You will work and pay until the debt is paid. Will this happen? In a practical sense no, but it could. The best way to avoid the problem is to drive carefully and not become involved in a wreck.

It doesn't seem fair, does it?

Or is it? What about the young father who is no longer able to work to provide for his family because of your negligence or carelessness? A 25-year-old man who was making $40,000 a year and looking forward to another 40 years in his career field, now can no longer work due to your actions. How is he going to make up his lost salary to take care of his family? Assuming he prospers in his work and his salary increases a nominal eight per cent per year until it reaches $100,000 annually, his total lost salaries will amount to $3.5 million.

On top of this $3.5 million loss, add his medical bills for the accident and any recurring medical problems he may suffer later in life. You can see how one accident caused by negligence or carelessness can easily cost millions of dollars.

Driving a car is not a right; it is a privilege. Additionally, you must always act responsibly behind the wheel of a car. Too often police charge teenagers and young adults in accidents that have caused permanent handicap or death to others only because they were *irresponsible*. The young people were doing things such as texting, talking on their cell phones, interacting with friends, or operating unsafe cars.

Many accidents caused by some young people changed other peoples' lives forever. Families have lost loved ones, individuals ended up in wheelchairs for life, and those who caused the accidents had their future dreams and hopes littered all over the roadside.

Driving a car is serious business. If you don't treat it as such, you may hurt others, and yourself. When people operate motor vehicles carelessly or recklessly, especially at high speeds, they may not understand the laws of physics. At high speeds, if the car hits something solid, the destruction of the vehicle is almost instantaneous.

People's lives change in less time than what it takes to read this sentence. And once it happens, there is no going back. There is no "fixing it." There are no "do overs."

I often think back to my high school classmates and one girl in particular. My friend was doing everything right; she was taking her child to day care. She was in traffic with a green light and someone else's careless operation of a cement truck killed her child. She was severely injured and never recovered from those injuries. She was paralyzed and lived a very long time, years in fact, but still died young.

When it comes to driving, please be careful. As

mentioned, your driving record can either close or open doors.

I know I sound like your mom or dad, but here's the truth: They know what they are talking about when it comes to life. There is a lot to be said about the phrase, "Been there, done that." Your parents, like many, have already gone through what you are now experiencing. They know. Some of those parents are praying you don't make the same mistakes they did. And many hope you achieve more in your life than what they did.

What is important to remember about driving and cars is that you must be responsible. The real secret about cars is that we have to have them, but you must be careful.

Chapter 9 – You have to save

"The most powerful force in the universe is compound interest."
– Albert Einstein

Would you like to know the real secret to success? In a single word, it is "discipline."

Savings, combined with compound interest, can make anyone financially healthy. The key is discipline. As with any program, you have to design your savings plan, determine your monthly investment, and then stick with the plan.

More than likely, you have heard your parents talk about how important it is to save. The problem with some families is that it is little more than talk; for a person to learn how to save effectively, they must actually see savings in action and they need to be able to measure the results of the savings program.

For many, the idea of saving started with a twenty-five cent allowance. Their parents gave them a quarter and told them to save a nickel from each quarter. The parents wanted to train their children to save a portion of their allowance. In theory, it is a fine idea. After a whole year collecting quarters each week, the child would have $13. Of that, if they saved a nickel a week, they would have saved $2.60 in the year.

To learn how to save effectively, you have to see real results. You have to understand the concepts of saving—with and without interest. You should also understand the idea of simple interest compared to compound interest. If you are saving for the short term, simple interest is fine. On the other hand, if you are saving for some serious money, you definitely want to investigate banks, credit unions, or investment companies offering compounded interest accounts.

Many people have a weak understanding about savings, savings accounts, or interest. For example, if you save $50 a month underneath your mattress, after 12 months you have $600. If you took your money down to the bank and put it into an account with a simple interest of three percent, at the end of 12 months, instead of $600 you would have $608. Three percent is not a lot of interest, but as some have said, it is better than nothing. Leave the money in the account and continue to add $50 a month, after three years, your account will grow to $1881, after four years, it will reach $2546, and at the five-year anniversary, it will total $3232. If, during that time you continued to stuff a $50 bill under your mattress, you would have only $3000.

Without doubt, saving money in a compound interest bearing account is the most important thing you can do for yourself. Be mindful that as the balance of the account grows, the amount of money earned in interest increases.

If you can purchase whatever you want with cash, you can save a lot of money in the end. As an example, a used car valued at $5,000 purchased on credit with $500 down with the balance financed at eight percent for three years will cost another $576 in interest. This brings the total cost of the car to $5576 ($500 down + $4500 loan + $575 interest) resulting in a monthly payment for three years of $141.

How long would take to save $5,000 for the car? Don't forget the other costs of the car, such as gasoline, minor maintenance, and insurance. Depending on how much you drive, gasoline might be as much as $150 a month. Minor maintenance will probably run about $30, while insurance might average as much as or more than $250 per month.

This brings your monthly expense for transportation to a total of $430. Add to this the car payment of $141 and your monthly cost for driving your car is $571. If you could save $571 per month, it would take a little over eight months to buy your car outright. If you could only save the monthly cost of the car, $141, it would take about three years to pay cash. It seems like a grind, but consider that by saving and buying with cash, you will not have to pay the $576 interest on the loan.

With other purchases, especially a major purchase such as a house, saving is the most important part of your success. First, you should absolutely buy a house.

For many, a house is more than a home—it is a very fine savings program in itself. Remember, though, these are rules that worked very well for your parents and their friends. The rules for today and tomorrow may be different, and they continue to change still.

Real estate prices have continued to edge up at a nominal rate of a little less than five percent per year from 1940 to the year 2000. In some years, the increase in home values was phenomenal while in others, increases were modest. What is important to understand is the idea that home ownership is one key to developing wealth, as long as the market doesn't crash as it did in 2008.

To put this in better perspective, take this example: Assume that at age 18, you begin saving for your first home. Over the course of six years, you save $18,000 in a compounded interest account. Using that money as a down payment on a modest $100,000 house, the mortgage payment is only $465 for a 30 year mortgage with a 5.5 percent interest rate. Over the next 10 years, the value of the house increases. At the same time, the balance on the mortgage decreases by about $16,000. What this means is you can sell your house and put anywhere from $50,000 to $100,000 in your back pocket after paying off the original loan.

Once you sell your first home, you can buy another house and start the process all over again—with bigger numbers! By using this technique, you can make quite a bit of money over the course of a lifetime.

You could also decide not to sell the first home, but rather, start renting it. As long as you keep it rented for a rental rate higher than your mortgage, you will maintain a positive cash flow. This allows you to continue paying down the mortgage, which increases the equity in your property.

Anyone can do this. A friend of mine started this plan about 35 years ago. He has bought and sold about 40 homes over the period and today, he is more than a millionaire.

Another method of possibly becoming a millionaire is by investing. To be successful, you have to understand and really know what you are doing. Additionally, you might need a fairly large chunk of change to start. What follows is a very basic look at the market and should you choose to work with the stock market, here is a word of advice—you need serious study on the subject. Working in the market requires a whole lot more education than these few introductory paragraphs.

If you buy stocks and the company stays in business, you have an account worth something. For example, if you buy 100 shares of Apple (AAPL) at $460 per share, it would cost $46,000 (see what I mean by a "fairly large" chunk of change?). Once bought, you now have an account worth $46,000 — as long as the value of the stock remains at $460 per share.

If the stock falls, it will be something less. If it falls to $450 per share, the value of your account will lose $1,000 ($10/share x 100). On the other hand, if the price of the stock goes up $20, you have just made $2,000. Oh by the way, don't forget that you will have to pay taxes on your investment gains.

There are other, cheaper stocks with which you can get into the market. New companies are getting off the ground almost daily. You can purchase some stocks at reasonable rates of less than $1. Be aware the lower the stock price, the smaller the fluctuation in price. Remember that when the average price for the market goes up three percent, the change in a $2 stock amounts to six cents whereas a three percent change in AAPL at $460 per share is $14. To reiterate the message, you have to become *very well-educated to trade in the market*.

Here is a word of warning. You can make a lot of money relatively quickly in the market. You can also lose everything you own, literally, in less than a minute — if you don't know what you're doing.

Always remember, the higher the risk, the higher the reward. For some, the risk is something they really must have as part of the thrill of the trade. You must have a plan going into the trade, you must know how much you can make, and you need to know your exit strategy.

This is another way of saying you need to know how to get out of the trade before it is too late.

Chapter 10 – Credit and credit cards

All right, now you're out of school and on your own. What's next?
Credit cards, of course!
Whoa! Hold on there, pardner! Careful! You are about to enter one of the most dangerous of the Danger Zones!

When it comes to credit, you really have to be careful. Credit used properly is one of your best tools for navigating the financial world. Used carelessly or improperly, however, it can ruin your life.

Most do not know how to use credit. Many feel as though holding a credit card is license to buy anything, anytime they want. The truth is: Yes, … and no.

The bottom line is the same as always before. If you can afford it, buy it. If not, don't. Having a credit card merely gives you other purchase and payment options. The mass media monster takes in too many young people with the advertising garbage they feed the public about the wonderful benefits of a particular card. If you were to listen to those "marketing experts" and their ads, it would lead you to believe *all* money is easy to come by.

Because of aggressive advertising, many apply for their cards and immediately start spending. It is very easy to be irresponsible with credit card purchases; it is also easy to buy almost anything you want on credit. That's what the credit card companies *want* you to do.

The next thing they would like you to do is make only the minimum monthly payment. What they won't tell you is that by making only the minimum payment, it will take you 15 to 20 years, or more, to pay off your debt. In the meantime, they collect a *phenomenal* amount of money from you in interest.

As an example, if in January 2016, a young person ran his or her credit balance on a particular card up to $3,500 with the intent of paying off the loan at $75 per month, he or she would be surprised at how long it will take to pay off the loan. At an interest rate of 18 percent, the holder of the loan will make the last payment in September 2022. Amazingly, the cost of the loan will amount to $2,557! Incredibly, to borrow $3,500, it will cost 73 percent of the original amount. It will probably be more because will spend more money to live during the time you are paying this debt. To better visualize just the costs and payments, take a look at the following table:

	Year-end Principle balance	Year-end Interest paid
2016	$3,206	$607
2017	$2,856	$549
2018	$2,436	$481
2019	$1,935	$389
2020	$1,335	$300
2021	$618	$183
2022	$0	$48

Table 4. Year-end balance and interest paid on a $3,500 loan taken out on January 1, 2016 with payments of $75 per month. Interest will total $2,557 and it will take six years and nine months to pay off.

Here is another way of looking at this. Whatever you need that is priced at $3,500 will actually cost you about $6,000 — the cost of the original item plus the interest paid to carry the loan. No matter how you slice it, the principle plus the interest ads up to a very hefty price tag.

Back in Chapter 5, I referred to using, or rather, not using your credit card for meals. Can you use cards for eating? Sure, you can! All you have to do is whip it out after eating, hand it to the waitress or waiter, and in a few minutes you will have paid for your meal without using cash. No problem, right?

Well, yes, there is a problem. Do this eight, nine times a month at $25 a pop and you can see that it will run up a debt quickly ($25 x 9 = $225). If you don't have $225 right away, you can float yourself a loan through the credit card company and trust me, they like it when you do that. They really like it if your interest rate is up above 15 percent or higher.

Do this for about four months ($225 x 4 = $900) and now you will have a pretty large balance on your card if you have not been paying it off with generous monthly payments. After a few months, you are going to owe quite a bit on your account with nothing to show for it. At least if you buy a television, DVD player, computer, or something else, you can watch it, play it, or use it at the same time you are making payments on your credit card.

Meals on the other hand, well, let's just say they're gone...

This is why it is important to develop good saving habits while you are young (remember everything you read in Chapter 9). While it takes six years and nine months to pay off $3,500, it takes about half that time to save the same amount. Sure, you have to do without until you have the money, but you will not have the pressure to make a payment on time.

This makes for a far less stressful life than being under the gun for payments, something many fail to realize. For those who succumb to the lure of buying now and paying later, they will live their lives with a large payment due on the fifth (or whatever day of the month) the payment is due.

Remember that credit card companies want to keep that dirty little secret. If you only make the minimum payment, sometimes, the interest you pay will be more than the loan itself.

As you start your financial life, you must have at least one credit card. There are some things you cannot buy with cash. For example, airline tickets — in addition to paying for a ticket to faraway destinations, the credit card doubles as a check on your identity. Ditto for renting a car or truck.

In addition to being able to buy airline tickets and rent vehicles, a credit card is a convenient way to make purchases. You don't have to walk around with a wad of cash in your back pocket. You can charge almost any purchase to any one of a number of major credit cards. But here's the secret trick! Pay off the balance every month.

If you pay off the balance when your credit card bill arrives, the bank will not charge interest on your purchases. This is similar to having a short loan for 30 days at a time. In essence, you are borrowing the money from the bank to use it interest-free during that month. Additionally, there are other benefits to using cards to purchase goods and services.

If you have a card that offers cash back incentives as you purchase your daily expenses, the card company returns a small percentage of your purchase price as a reward or incentive for using their card. For example, if you use your card for gasoline, your groceries, clothing, dining out, and other acquisitions that amount to $1500 or $1600 per month, with a two percent cash back award, the credit card company will credit your account with about $30. As long as you pay off the balance each month, you are ahead of the game —

particularly if your credit card company is paying back *three* percent. That amounts to about $400 per year they will pay — to you.

Something else to look for, and the only way you can find this is by reading the fine print, are any transaction fees. Another trick some card companies try to pull on the public is charging an "annual membership fee." This can be as much as $100, just for the privilege of carrying and using their card. You can probably find another company willing to issue you a card without charging such fees.

When it comes to choosing a card, here are a couple of other things to think about. First, limit the number cards you carry. You should also keep the total credit line to an amount you are comfortable with; you should easily be able to pay off your debt quickly, if needed.

Be aware that if you are late making your regular payment, the credit card company will probably slam you with a hefty late fee and increase your interest rate to an unacceptable level. You must always manage your credit properly by paying more than the minimum amount, as well as making payments before they are due. Do not get into the habit of paying your credit card bill at the last minute. If you pay late or insufficiently, they are going to penalize you and there is nothing you can do about it, because it is in the fine print.

Something else to think about with your credit cards is managing your receipts. Always keep your receipts in a safe place and when your bill comes in, reconcile the receipts against the bill immediately. If you find a discrepancy, report the problem to the card company right away.

This is important, particularly during these days of fraud and identity theft. The sooner you can report a fraudulent purchase, the easier the problem is to resolve (see the next chapter on identity theft). Another great habit to start is guarding your receipts; do not allow your personal information to get away from you.

To sum up the use of credit cards, don't overspend, take off the balance monthly, and watch your receipts.

Chapter 11 – Identity Theft

Wow! Now you're on your own. You can buy things, go anywhere, and do anything you want. Right? Yes! But only to a point.

There are some precautions you should and must take, just to be safe.

Safe? Safe *from what*, you ask?

Well, now that you're on your own, you have to take over the job of looking out for yourself. And we're not talking about the boogeyman or avoiding dark allies, here. What we're talking about is identity theft.

Identity thieves are very resourceful at stealing your information. This is why you have to be careful about guarding your bank account, credit card, health, and other information. These deadbeats will actually rummage through your garbage to get the information they need to suck money out of your bank account, run up your credit cards, and obtain a host of other financial or private services in your name.

All of those free offers are coming from companies who want your information. You are the "offer," if you give them your information. Your private information will be theirs to use as they please. Some will use it in marketing, others will sell your information to the highest bidder, and almost all of them will not protect your numbers as they should be protected.

As a young person, you hold a lot of promise in your future life. If you are starting out in a new career, you stand the chance of making money. Possibly a lot of money. It is something that attracts potential employers to you. Unfortunately, these are the same qualities that attract thieves.

So, what can you do to protect yourself? First, shred every piece of mail you receive with your printed name and address on it—especially if it has any account information accompanying it.

Shredding your mail is especially important if it contains any of those "free" offers—in particular, those from banks or credit card companies that include account information on pre-printed checks.

Why credit card companies and banks continue to jeopardize their clients in this manner goes beyond common sense. Certainly, at some point, a group of victims will file a class-action lawsuit against companies engaging in these practices that open their customers to the possibility of devastating financial disaster.

If a company mails anything to your address carrying your private information, you cannot afford just "to throw it out." By the way, when I talk of shredding, I am not talking about tearing up mail into tiny pieces; I am talking about shredding it. With a shredder. Preferably a crosscut shredder if you can afford it. The best thing you can do for yourself to protect your financial interests is the practice and habit of never throwing out any personal information.

If the information you throw out remains intact, anyone can use it to buy goods or services in your name. Unfortunately, you may be liable for those losses if you fail to take reasonable precautions to protect yourself.

What is a reasonable precaution? Notification of the fraudulent charge against your account in a reasonable period of time. There's that word again—"reasonable." Now all you have to do is define "reasonable." We live in a truly magnificent time. Who would ever have thought we would be able to check all of our financial accounts at once—with the simple touch of a computer key stroke. This quickly allows you to thoroughly monitor all of your finances at once. Computers and the Internet are some of the most valuable tools we possess in the fight against identity theft. Unfortunately, these same tools also aid the bad guys. Stay cognizant that to protect yourself, you should check all of your accounts at least weekly—maybe even daily.

So, how do you know if someone stole your information? Ah, there's the trick.

The first, most likely thing you will notice are withdrawals from your bank account that you know you did not initiate or authorize. You might get bills from companies or medical offices for services that you did not use. A company you do business with might notify you their files were hacked and your private information was lost in the breach. And here is one of the worst, a new ID theft technique showing up of late—the IRS calls and notifies you that two or more returns were filed in your name, or that you have income from a company at which you were not employed. This crime emphasizes the need for never allowing your social security number out.

The sooner you discover the fraud against your name, the easier it is to clean up. If you did not know this, it takes an average of 700 hours of research, letter writing, telephone calls, and one-on-one discussions for an ID theft victim to clear his or her name. That is an awful lot of time and effort to fix a problem you can easily avoid with a few good practices.

As long as you keep up the good prevention practices, you should be OK. If you protect your name, address, and personal account information, you make the thieves' job much more difficult; as a result, they will probably leave you alone. If you are hard to victimize, the predators will pass you by for easier prey. It is the law of survival, in the jungle or on the streets-and even in cyberspace.

What do you do if they get you? First, don't panic. Have a plan ready to execute and gain comfort from that plan. Let's start with the most common occurrence. A stolen wallet or purse.

The first thing to do is to contact the Federal Trade Commission. The FTC identity theft hot line is 877-438-4338. By calling this number, you can file a complaint and start the process of alerting the world that you are a legitimate victim of ID theft. The FTC does not resolve problems, but their involvement may lead to law enforcement action and conviction of the thief.

Next, call the police. If you lost your wallet or purse, or if someone stole your information, it is important to get an official police report filed for the loss. There is an important reason for having a police report. If the police arrest the "bad guy" for some other crime and he or she is carrying your identification, which ID do you think they will turn over to the police? Yep, you got it — if they have your ID, that's the ID they will give to the authorities when they have to produce an ID.

What do you think the likelihood the deadbeat will show for court? Yep, that's right — not likely. The authorities will then issue an arrest warrant for the deadbeat. Oops, right again! He didn't use his name, he used yours! So guess whose name will be on the arrest warrant? If the police pull you over for a broken taillight or other insignificant reason months later, there is a good chance you may spend the night in jail after they mistakenly identify you as the criminal.

If you have a copy of the original police report showing you were the victim of identity theft, it might help you to some degree. There are no guarantees; you may still find yourself down at the police station. However, a copy of the original police report will help. Be prepared, though, to be detained by the authorities while they sort out the mess. And that is what it is—a mess.

Beyond notifying the police, the next thing you must do is notify the credit-reporting bureaus. You may hear that reporting to one will suffice, that they will in turn, notify the others.

Now, as you make your way down the wormhole of problems caused by the thief, keep meticulous records. For each person you talk with over the phone, record their name, the date and time of the call, and the notes of the information discussed. Also, remember that solving the ID theft problem will probably take months, maybe years. Use certified mail to send any letters and before you send them, keep photocopies of the communication.

You should also place a security freeze on all of your credit files with the credit reporting agencies. You will have to contact each individually to do this, and the contact information is available at the end of this chapter.

Now this is important and it is the reason for monitoring all accounts that pop up in your name. You need to contact each company where a thief has opened a fraudulent account in your name. If you do this quickly, you may avoid the lion's share of fraudulent charges taken out in your name. If you find any accounts opened against your name, close and block each one.

One thing you can do to track fraudulent activity is check your credit reports. You can obtain credit reports from all three of the agencies and should you find anything you do not recognize, take action immediately. Remember that new activity can take as long as six months to show up on the reports, so you have to continue monitoring the reports.

Also remember the old cliché—if you want a job done right, you should do it yourself. I can think of nothing more important than a security breach to which this might apply.

The three bureaus are Equifax, Experian, and Trans Union. You should contact all by telephone and in writing. Again, keep copies of all correspondence and notes on all telephone conversations. Make note of everyone you talk with or write. Contact information for each is:

Federal Trade Commission Identity Theft Hotline
877/ID-THEFT (877-438-4338)

Equifax fraud division
800-525-6285
P.O. Box 740250
Atlanta, GA 30374
www.fraudalerts.equifax.com

Experian fraud division
888-397-3742
P.O. Box 1017
Allen, TX 75013
www.experian.com/fraud

Trans Union fraud division
800-680-7289
P.O. Box 6790
Fullerton, CA 92634
www.transunion.com/personal-credit

If you feel as if all of this is a pain in your rear, you are correct. However, as long as there is opportunity in the world for good, there is also going to be that for bad. Thieves have been with us since the beginning of time.

You just have to stay on your guard.

Chapter 12 – Do you want to get a job or start a career?

Most high school and many college students are anxious to graduate and start working. They cannot wait to make money and be on the way to bigger and better things. However, most still have to figure out a few things along the way.

For instance, what is a job? What is a career? Are the two synonymous? Or are they different? When you start working after graduation, which will make you happier? A job? Or a career? Do you know the difference between the two?

One day I was sitting at lunch with a friend, an airline pilot. We were discussing the condition of the airline industry. The airlines, as with other industries, have had a series of difficulties over the past decades. For some of the time, my friend had been on the roller coaster ride. As with many airline pilots, he had been with one company and then another and yet another as different companies declared bankruptcy, ceased operations all together, or furloughed pilots in an effort to stave off financial ruin.

Overlooking the banks of the St. Johns River, he said, "You know, I have the best job in the world, but my career sucks." As a flier myself who had elected not to join the airlines, I knew exactly what he meant.

In life, the opposite condition can also exist. You can have a great career while stuck in a terrible job. It boils down to getting what you want out of life. It is easier to be in a terrible job in a great career than vice versa. If you have chosen a terrible job in a good career field, you can change jobs. It is a little more difficult to change careers.

The question you have to ask at this juncture in your life is, what do you want to do? What will make you happy? Something else to consider is where you are in your life. If you're reading this book as a tenth grader, you need to go get a job. If you are into your senior year, it is time to start thinking about careers. If you are in college, particularly your last couple of years, you should be well on your way to your career.

Now, what if you're in your senior year of college and you have decided the career field you have chosen is not for you? Have you wasted time in college? Is it possible you may have exhausted a lot of money for nothing during that time? The good solid answer to these questions is —

maybe—it depends on your outlook and what you consider a waste.

As you move from childhood into adulthood, you will pass through a time of discovery. Some of you will have parents who will help you take a year off during this "gap" between high school and college. You may discover much during this time. Some of the things you may find could include your passion for life, what you will want to do for your life's work, and hopefully, find a soul mate with whom to share all of your discoveries.

If you are one of those lucky enough to be able to take a year after high school, use that time wisely. Find your passion, create something you can work with, help others.

If you are in the beginning of your time in high school, this is a good place to start thinking about what you are going to do to make your money. You have to have money of course, but the question becomes—how will you make your money. After all, there are as many ways to make money as there are fish in the ocean. The important idea about bringing home the bacon is how you prefer to get it home and cooked.

The preference we're talking about is your choice of work: Do you lean toward just having a job, or are you looking for a career? The difference between a job and a career is preparation. Jobs typically require little or no training, while a career can involve extensive college or on-the-job training.

When working on a job, if you tire of what you are doing, they lay you off, or the boss fires you, it is easier to switch to another job. A change in a career, on the other hand, is a bit more difficult, should a change become necessary.

Here is something else to think about when it comes to jobs and careers—some people are content working a job while others would never consider working outside of their chosen career field. It really is a matter of preference.

What each of you reading this book needs to determine is this: What do you prefer? Will you be happy working in only one career field, or would you prefer to go from one job to another? And here is the real bomb drop: Are there other ways to make money other than working a job or training for any one career field?

The answer to that question is an absolute, resoundingly loud—YES!

The trick is figuring out how to make money legally, without working in the traditional methods. This requires effort, but is well worth it. A few who did this actually created careers for themselves. Again, the question becomes one of what will make you the happiest in your work? Your life?

You definitely must have money shortly after graduating from high school. For most, this means getting a job. However, here is the "Catch-22" of the situation. You must have experience to get a job, and you need a job to get experience... (The phrase Catch-22 comes from the novel of the same name by Joseph Heller. He came up with the concept that you had to be insane to fly in combat and if you were, you didn't have to fly, but once you again realized flying in combat was insane, that meant you were sane again, and you had to fly. Read the book, it will definitely make you think and therefore, much more intelligent.)

Once a company hires you into a job, the next hardest thing you have to do is to ... keep your job. Sometimes, particularly at entry-level positions, the work can be boring and tedious. You will probably tire of your job quickly. It will seem as though you are doing the same thing every day, day in and day out, which of course, you are. After becoming bored, it is very tempting to walk off the job. Some people do. But remember; you still have to pay your bills.

So what do you do if you become bored with your job? You must figure out for yourself what you want to do that drives your passion. If you find this, you will never be bored at your job, or in your career. It may even drive you to start your own business, which will bring you considerably more satisfaction and reward than you can possibly imagine.

As previously noted, the difference between a job and a career is preparation and training. For most jobs, training might be as short as one day; preparation for a career, conversely, can take years. For instance, to work as an ophthalmologist you have to complete medical school, specialized medical training dealing with the eyes, complete a residency, and then set up your office. These are things you're not going to do overnight. Once completed, more than likely you are not going to change careers.

While starting a career may involve years of preparation, there are other benefits to being in a career field rather than just working jobs. The first is pay. While it is not always true, working in a career field usually pays better than jobs. In either a job or a career, if you are working for a company rather than yourself, you're going to have to be concerned with asking for raises.

You will discover most companies do not grant pay increases automatically. Many will link your income directly to your job performance. If you do well, you'll probably get a bump in pay. If not, your paycheck will remain flat.

OK, here's a little more information you might need about the working world.

In many instances, there is no longer loyalty between the company and you, the employee. During your grandparents' prime working years, and to a degree your parents, the conventional wisdom was to do well in school, graduate, get a job with a great company, and stay with them forever. During the 1920s and through the late 1960s, this idea worked well.

It worked well because companies valued their employees. The employees knew this, realized this, felt good about it, and knew that if they did well in their jobs, the company would prosper. If the company did well, they would pass down compensation to the workers in the form of increased wages or bonuses. This in turn, encouraged the employees to work harder for the company. When the employees worked harder, they had a sense they were working harder not for the company, but for themselves.

Because the employees worked so hard, many companies prospered. CEOs, presidents, and business owners realized their prosperity was the direct result of their loyal employees. Consequently, they took care of their people and the employees made certain they did right by their companies.

Unfortunately, this is no longer the working model in today's business world.

In these modern times, for a worker to acquire a significant bump in pay, they must leave one company and move to another. Another way to view this is that you may have to quit one job to get ahead. Here's the trick—don't leave one position before you have secured the next.

The reason for having to do this is because most companies now only provide cost of living raises of two to four percent annually. With the cost of living going up about 3.5 percent per year, some employees can't even keep up. So, to get a real increase in salary, you have to go out and find another company that values you for your experience and is willing to pay more than your current employer. Or, start your own company.

Your grandparents would never have a thought of getting a job and leaving the company within two or three years. The reality of today is that college graduates will have worked two or three jobs within their first decade out of college. Now, a word of caution: Never leave one job before you have secured the next. Always have a firm grasp on the brass ring before leaping.

Here is more important information about moving from one job to another. Talk with your current boss or supervisor; if they are aware another company is about to hire you away for a significantly higher salary, they may be inclined to match the other company's offer—just to keep you. If they do, you have a decision to make—stay where you are familiar with the operating procedures and where you have friends, or move to a new environment.

If you leave, do not make the mistake of "burning bridges." Whenever leaving one job, you should do so professionally, in order to return to the position if needed.

Chapter 13 – Are you ready for college?

Are you ready to start college? Believe it or not, some students really aren't prepared to begin serious academic study immediately after high school. This is the time some parents will sponsor their children through the "gap" year, that time between school and college. This is a good, traditional time to say, travel America, or ride trains throughout Europe. Bear in mind this is only a good option for those young people with "street smarts," the kind of intellect that will allow them to survive on their own.

Going to college might be the best thing for you, but then again, maybe not. You have to think about the reasons why you would go to college. It's to make more money, right? Are you sure you are going to make more money if you attend college? Could you make more, over your lifetime, if you were to start working right away in a trade? Have you "run the numbers?" Do you have the knowledge to create a small business? Is it possible you might be successful with computers, music, writing, software, or some other creative endeavour?

Now, don't get me wrong, I believe education is the most important thing everyone should acquire. However, sometimes becoming educated in these times might not involve traditional classrooms in colleges and universities; today, we can access a great deal of information by way of the Internet with PCs, iPads, Kindles, smartphones, and more. Oh yes, don't forget there are still those other ancient methods of obtaining information—through books located at various libraries throughout many communities. (See my comments about William Lear in my message to your parents.)

I played by all the rules they told me to follow when I was young. They said, "Go to college." I did. I started working professionally afterward and then went into the military. While I was doing all this, "they" were changing all the rules in the working world. Suddenly, the career I thought I would make a lot of money in went belly-up. Additionally, the business world rewrote the way they did business.

While I believed I would have made more money by now in my lifetime, I have friends who have done extremely well—friends who never went to college. Rather than spending the time and money attending a university, they started businesses and corporations, or began working in the trades. At the same time, you also need to realize that I have friends who did go to college, chose very critical professions, and their time and money spent in school allowed them to make much more money each year afterward.

If you are not ready, maybe you should not go to college—yet. Maybe you should have a gap year of self-realization. Eventually, you should go to college, but now might not be *your time*. Students who are ready for college usually do well once they are there. Those not ready typically end up with low grades, sometimes flunking out altogether.

If you are not ready for the serious investment of time, money, and effort to pursue a college degree, maybe you should do something else for a while. During the time you are away from school, you will begin to see the importance of college. You will gain part of this invaluable insight from working a variety of low-paying jobs that you have to work in order to survive.

While flipping burgers, mowing lawns, working in retail or in a shop, you quickly realize many of these lower paying positions are little more than "stepping-stone" jobs, jobs which will never satisfy your need for happiness.

What typically happens while working one of these jobs is this: One day, you stop and look around at what you are doing and the people with whom you are working. Then it hits you like a ton of bricks—you could be doing better. You realize that to do what you really want to do and be truly happy, you have to go back to school.

This is a common experience among older college students. It is the sudden realization that propels them through school with higher grades. In short, these students become successful because they *want to* and *choose to succeed.*

Remember this very important concept: What you think about, you bring about. If you think you are going to succeed, you will. If you believe you will fail, you will do that, instead. Keep positive thoughts and energy!

Another point about going to college is that some professions require a college degree. If you wish to be the first person to Mars (and I am not being facetious here, someone in your generation really will be the first human to walk on the red planet), you have to study math and science on the level of a PhD.

To be successful in college, you have to want it. You have to be ready to learn. You must absolutely be dedicated to the idea of success — and not just in school. If you are successful in life, it makes sense that you will be successful in everything you do.

If you are one of those who is not ready for college right after high school, or are still "searching" for yourself, take the time to figure out life. But maybe not in college — unless you are independently wealthy. If that is the case, you probably don't need to read this book, unless you're reading it for pleasure or curiosity.

Going to college before you are ready is really an expensive proposition. Tuition, books, lab and other fees are a lot to pay, but you will also have to pay those other expenses required of life. Things like rent, utilities, car payments, food, and gas.

Living expenses for one person out on their own can easily exceed $20,000, maybe $25,000 a year or more, even while living frugally. Now add another $15,000 to $50,000 a year for educational expenses. Total costs can quickly add up to a quarter million dollars or more for four years of college.

This is why you have to be ready for serious academic study when you begin your collegiate career. If you are not, you can, and probably will, waste a lot of money while you are trying to get your act together.

As I aged (physically, mentally, and spiritually), I came to the realization that for many, the only way they will be happy is if they create a way to take charge of their lives. They need to make their way through life on their own, especially financially. I must say that I really wish I had learned this lesson when I was in my 20s, rather than later in life.

There are some who might understand this..., However, most do not. If you can create your own wealth from your own efforts, *you will be* in charge of your life. *Forever*. This is not to say you won't be working hard, because you will. On your own, you will work harder than you can imagine, much harder than if you were working for someone else or a corporation. However, once you have acquired a taste of your own success, whether you have a college degree or not, you are going to be far ahead of your high school classmates.

One thing about studying well in school is the development of critical thinking skills. A person who has exceptional critical thinking skills is a person who has mastered math. The mastery of math is one of the most critical aspects of life.

If you have those skills, you can analyze your best path to wealth. If you graduate from high school and start working on building your wealth, you will begin making money right away. A person who goes to college, however, delays the start of making money and, possibly, accrues a degree of debt in student loans.

The bottom line is this question: How much money can you make over your lifetime, regardless of education, student debt, jobs, and business pursuits. Then there is the most important concept—happiness. If you love what you are doing, you are going to be a happy person.

So if you are not ready to continue your education, what do you do? Get a job, join the military, come up with a great idea (see chapters 7, 14, and 16). Whatever you do, try doing something that will help others. Be a positive force in life; don't be a drain. If you have an entrepreneurial spirit or an inventive mind, you might develop something that may provide you with a serious income for the rest of your life while benefiting others.

As I said, be a positive force and try to figure out a way to give back to society while you are making your fortunes, going to school, or trying to figure out what you what you are supposed to be doing while you are here.

Chapter 14 – The military option

Want to travel the world and get some great job training at the same time? In others words, earn while you learn? If you do, one of your best options is the military.

Many might object to the idea of military service, but without the sacrifices of those who have gone before us, we would not be this great nation. History is another very important subject each of us needs study, and to remember.

Some think you cannot learn decent job skills in the service. Be aware that you can receive some of the best on the job training (OJT) in the latest technological fields of today.

If you are one of those who question the "whole military thing," you should probably think again. And perhaps do a little research and ask a few questions.

Each branch of the services has similar entry requirements, but today is not like in the old days. There are more candidates, really great candidates, from which military leaders can choose. In World War II, it was easy for a young person who was in trouble with the law to get a second chance by volunteering for the military. Today, however, if you have a serious legal problem in your background, you may not be able to enlist in the Army, the Navy, the Air Force, or the Marines.

You also need good grades to accompany your high school diploma. Yes, if you have a GED, you can join the military; however, as with many things, the actual diploma opens many more doors with greater opportunities and career directions. The more you really know, the better your career choices.

In addition to your overall general knowledge, you must also be in shape. Each branch has their independent physical test requirements, but the first thing you have to do is pass a standard medical examination. Then you can start thinking about the fitness requirements, which many seem to dread, but isn't that bad.

The reason the military requires candidates to pass a physical fitness test should be obvious. Many of the duties performed by military members take strength and endurance. Consequently, the military designed each physical fitness test (PFT) to test cardiovascular endurance, strength, and mobility. Each service has designed their own tests and standards, dependent on the requirements of their individual missions.

In general, the military branches have entry requirements consisting of a body mass measurement, pushups, sit ups, and a run component. The body mass index (BMI) for the Army and Navy is 22; for the Air Force, 20; and 18 for the Marines.

The pushup requirement for each service is slightly different, but the average is 30 to 40 within a two-minute time limit. Sit ups are similar with 40 to 60 in two minutes.

Of course, the requirement to be in good shape is part of the job if you are in the military. Many times, it is the strength and endurance capability of the soldiers, sailors, marines, and airmen that solve problems on many humanitarian missions around the world where our military has helped Americans and the citizens of other nations cope with natural disasters and political situations.

Once enlisted, each branch of the services will trust you with a great amount of responsibility—almost immediately. It is far better to be in charge of hundreds or thousands of dollars of equipment and making a good salary, compared to flipping burgers, digging ditches, or doing retail work.

The military can truly offer you a career while civilian companies can only provide entry-level jobs. Yes, there is a possibility you could get hurt or killed serving your country. But you could also accidentally die while crossing a busy highway walking to your local job.

The military will give you serious responsibility from the beginning. You will not have those same opportunities in the civilian sector. And the truth of the matter is this: Working in the military is a lot more fun, immensely more challenging, and incredibly more rewarding.

When it comes to the idea of going into the military, you must view it from different perspectives. For one, is the military right for you? Secondly, are you right for the military? It does take a special kind of person to be a part of a military organization. Not everyone is capable.

One question many ask is, "Will I die in a war?" That's a good question. Maybe. Probably not. That's why I say some people are good for the military, others are not.

While it is not in the job description, there exists the possibility you may have to follow through with your orders into an armed conflict. After all, it is one of the functions of the military. Many young Americans since 1776 have known and understood the importance of serving. For the most part however, working in the military is very much like working anywhere else in any other industry.

There is phenomenal opportunity in the military in every vocation imaginable. Think of all the jobs in civilian life. The Army, Navy, Air Force, Marines, and Coast Guard must also have each of those jobs accomplished within their ranks. Essentially, the military needs bakers, computer specialists, photographers, secretaries, cooks, intelligence specialists, data entry clerks, bankers, firemen, construction workers, policemen, radio technicians, aircraft mechanics, doctors, pilots, nurses, small boat operators, and more.

The difference between doing any of these jobs "on the outside," or in the military, is that the military gives you far more opportunities earlier in your career. This will allow you to excel in your profession and gain more experience than your civilian counterparts.

Another great thing about military service is preparation for college, both financially and emotionally. The military has many different and great educational plans to help both active duty personnel and veterans attain their college educational goals. For students not quite ready for school who might need a little discipline in their lives, the military option is a great way to go.

For some in the enlisted ranks, college is merely a break between their enlisted service and their commissioned service as an officer. These are the high school graduates who quickly saw the benefits of service, really liked what they were doing, and became aware of the need for education. After completing their baccalaureate degrees and/or masters, they returned to serve their country with brass on their shoulders.

Typically, these are the officers who return to very interesting jobs in the military. A few have gone on to positions of historical importance.

Here is something else to think about when it comes to college and the military. One of the very best options a young person has today is the possibility of attending one of the service academies. For the Army, that would be West Point; the Air Force has The Air Force Academy in Colorado; Navy midshipmen and potential Marine second lieutenants attend Annapolis; and the Coast Guard has its own academy in New London, CT.

For those who desire to serve in the military and obtain their college education at the same time, this is the best course they can follow. This is no easy path, however, as the only way into one of the academies is by way of a congressional nomination. The latter part of the process includes multiple medical and physical tests.

The first obstacle, obtaining the congressional nomination, requires the best and brightest of applicants. Additionally, they must be sincerely interested *in serving* the nation. After passing the aptitude, medical, and physical testing, what follows is four years of intensive academic study and physical training.

For retirement purposes, the four years spent attending one of the service academies measures as part of service. A young person entering one of the academies at the age of 18 can retire from the military with a lifetime pension at the age of 38. That sounds old to some who will read this, but rest assured, 38 is young enough to start an entirely new career.

The education provided by the academies is worth about half a million dollars. It is an education free to those who choose, elect to compete, and then win, an appointment. Additionally, graduates from the academies find themselves working immediately after graduation in job fields many civilians could only dream of, or wish to obtain.

As a young person, if you think you would like to choose this route to the rest of your life, take note: You have to start right now, while you are in middle or high school. Remember when your parents and grandparents told you to make good grades? And to stay out of trouble? This is why. If you got into trouble, if your grades are low, or if you were too shy, there is little chance you could compete for one of these prestigious seats in any of the service academies.

If you are still in school and thinking about college, you should do the very best you can. Make yourself as competitive as possible for any school you might choose. It does not matter if you go to that school right after high school, or later in life. You will still be prepared and you will do well. You will also have some work and life experience to place on your resume, making yourself more attractive to higher paying jobs, or the university of your choice.

Chapter 15 – Leadership & Attitude

As you begin making your way into the world, look around and determine where you want to go. One thing that will help you get there is your ability as a leader. Yes, that's right—you have to be a leader.

Some people are natural born leaders, others have to develop their leadership skills, and then there are those who may never become a leader. Where do you fall on the measuring stick? Do you always want to take charge? Do you naturally fall into a leadership position? Or are you likely to shirk leadership responsibilities?

Have you ever heard of the term, locus of control? It is essentially the belief that we are either in control of our destinies, or not. The concept was developed in the mid-1950s by Julian B. Rotter. It is commonly used personality studies. Anyone with a strong sense of an internal locus of control, tend to believe that what happens to them in their lives is a direct result of their own actions. Essentially, they believe they are responsible for their own success, or failure. Leadership fits well into the idea of a strong internal sense of locus of control. Many in leadership positions truly believe they can determine the outcome of their efforts.

Leadership comes in all kinds of ways and formats. You might find yourself working as a member of a team contributing to the success of a project. You could also be the person tying others together on a particular job. You might find yourself as the individual organizing many to make things happen. It is all up to you.

There are many ways to acquire leadership skills. One is through management training programs with various companies. Universities also have excellent business programs. Another is through military training. Each has advantages and disadvantages.

Discipline is another aspect of leadership you must consider. You must force yourself to do what's needed to finish the job. As a leader, you must be able to do the job that you would delegate to others. Leadership and discipline are, after all, the essence of the entrepreneurial spirit.

Now, here is something else that is very important about being a leader.

You must have the right attitude.

Just because someone puts you in charge of a team, appoints you to round up a project, or assign you to accomplish a goal with a group of your peers, it does not mean you will be successful in leading others to the end goal.

Without the right attitude, people will not follow you.

There was a great story making its way around the Internet a while back about a restaurant manager who was a true leader. As he moved from one restaurant to the next for better pay and benefits, he often took the best of the wait staff from his current restaurant with him. Almost everyone he asked followed him to the new store because he was a leader with a great attitude, which made working for him fun.

He was well on his way to success when he made an error no one in the restaurant business should make late at night. He took out the garbage and did not make certain the door locked behind him when he returned. Robbers followed him in and unfortunately, they shot him.

Later, as he described it, the EMTs, doctors, and nurses were all telling him, "Hang in there! You're going to make it!" However, their eyes were saying, "So sorry, you are such a dead man."

Recognizing the situation for what it was, when a nurse asked him if he was allergic to anything, he motioned her to come closer. She did not hear.

Then, at the top of his lungs, he yelled, "The only thing I am allergic to are bullets!"

Everyone cracked up when they heard his proclamation and suddenly, the dynamics of the emergency room completely changed. Instead of working to make him comfortable while waiting for the inevitable, they really went to work to save his life. Consequently, he went on to recover, continue working in the restaurant business, and always made sure the back door was locked!

There are other things about leadership and attitude you should know. If you do not have the characteristics of a leader, you will not be successful. If you have a "stinky" attitude, no one will want to (pick any) 1) be around you, 2) will want to work with you, 3) will want to work for you, 4) will want you on their team, 5) will want to be in the same room with you... I think you are getting the picture.

Leadership and attitude are the important parts of the formula for success. Without them, there will be no success. And if there is no success, the void is filled with failure. Remember, though, failure is only a part of the equation for success. It is not a lasting condition.

Again, as it was pointed out in Chapter 3, it really is your choice...

Chapter 16 – The big bucks

Please, don't be one of those idealistic individuals who believe all of the rich in the world are horrible people. The truth is—some are, but most are not.

Here is something else very true about those "nasty rich people." They are the ones who provide the jobs for the masses. It is the rich who had guts enough to take the risks to make money. Many times, when the rich put plans into action to make money for themselves, they create jobs for others; it happens when they have to create factories or open shops, or create medical clinics in order to facilitate their own dreams and ambitions.

Recall the answer to the famous question, "Did you ever get a job from a poor person?"

Someone has to be rich, so why not you?

If you are serious about making a lot of money, here is another important concept: You must not, or should not, have "a job." For the most part, having a regular 9 to 5 job is a waste of time. You can work as hard and as long as you wish, but when it comes to making "big money," you are limiting how much money you can make while employed with another company.

To explain, a typical job will have you working 40 hours per week. With 52 weeks in a year, the average worker will be on the job 2080 hours (40 hours x 52 weeks). At the Federal minimum wage of $7.65 per hour, this equates to only $15,912 for the year. Even if you were making $15 an hour, your annual salary would only be $31,200 per year.

The problem is the hourly limitation. There are only 24 hours in a day and you can work only so many hours before you collapse. If you work hard and you work long hours overtime, you might be able to work 2500 or so hours in any given year.

Now, multiply those hours out by your hourly pay rate and you will realize the other limitation to how much you can make in one year. You should also realize that it is not only how much you make, you need to consider what you do with your income. It could be as important as the salary itself.

Here is something you should think about: The fallacy of the "big salary." This is particularly important to those of you reading this book who are about to graduate from college. Many companies have determined the best way around some of the Federal work regulations is to hire people on a fixed salary.

Take a look at this example between an hourly employee and a salaried "manager." Let's examine the differences in their lives and the money they actually make.

"Dave" is hired by the company as "a worker" at an hourly rate of $17.30, while "Ned" becomes "a manager" salaried at $36,000 a year. Both Dave and Ned have to work about 2,600 hours in the year because of the demands of their respective jobs.

Dave, as an hourly worker, gets paid time and a half for his overtime work. On the other hand, the company only pays Ned his salary.

In the end, Dave makes $49,650 or about $19.06 per hour. Ned, in his salaried position, works as hard and makes $36,000 for the year. Divided by the 2,600 hours he spent working to make the money, his actual hourly rate becomes $13.84

If you are really interested in making more than an average salary, you need to understand that working for anyone else will probably keep you from making your dreams come true. The sooner you learn this important lesson, the quicker you can make your dreams happen. And the quicker you make it happen, you will find more opportunities.

Also remember that if you are working for someone else, what you are doing is making money for them. While the boss makes more money, you keep pushing your "big payday" further into the future. In fact, working for your boss may jeopardize your chances of ever reaching your dreams and making a great living.

If you see a great opportunity, you have to jump on it. There is no question that you must have the time and opportunity to pursue your dreams; you can define opportunity as having the money, the facilities, or the people to help you make your dreams happen. Moreover, time is exactly what it is — a current or flow in which there is no chance to turn around and go "up river."

Once that time, or your chance, or a lifetime opportunity has passed, you can never go back and have a "do over." If you see a great prospect, you have to take a shot at it right then. Otherwise, it may be gone forever.

One place I have repeatedly seen the reality of this is at the airshows I enjoy attending throughout the nation. I have listened to more than a few individuals delude themselves into believing they could have flown jets "like those jet pilots up there," if only... If only they had gone to school, if only they had enlisted in the military, if only they had learned how to fly, if only... if only...

The truth of the matter is this: In order to fly those jets, you have to go out and really work at it. You have to *see* the opportunity and *take it!* If you let it pass you by, the chance you had is gone forever. This includes many things in life.

Here is another important caveat; you may fail. In fact, there is a high likelihood of your failure. However, your work will not be a complete failure if you learn from your mistakes and then make certain not to repeat them in your future projects and accomplishments. Keep this in mind; you cannot be a success without having a few failures along the way.

Many do not realize that failure is the key to success. Remember one of the famous people mentioned at the beginning of the book as being home schooled? Thomas Edison. How many times did he fail at developing the proper filament for the light bulb before he had success? Could he have given up? Might he have said, "This is too hard?" He could have quit, but he did not. Each failure along the way was a part of his success.

The trick to living life successfully and paying your bills while developing new projects, is to know when you have to work for others and knowing when you can go it on your own. As noted above, if you really want to make a lot of money, you have to work for yourself. Working for others only makes them richer.

This is also another important concept to remember—you will have far greater job satisfaction if you are the one calling the shots. If you are not dependent on someone else, a particular company, or a boss for your paycheck, you will have greater freedom to determine when you should work and when you can take it easy. Also, you don't have to ask anyone for time off, when you're the boss.

Something else to consider is that you will never have to ask anyone for a raise. The idea here is simple: If you need more money, just go out and determine what you have to do to get it.

If you think about it, you will have complete control over all aspects of your life. Remember, in order to do this you have to plan accordingly to make the money you believe you would like to make or need. Rest assured, in this time of the Internet, instantaneous communication, and online banking, we really can do anything we desire. This includes making money. Great gobs of money. An actual "money tree" may not exist, but there are some other things which come pretty close.

Just keep in mind that it still takes a lot of work, dedication, and motivation to achieve your dreams. For those willing to do the work, the rewards are phenomenal. You just have to go out and do it.

Now, here is another little secret that might help you achieve your goals.

Look to your left and to your right. Look in front of you and look behind. Do you see all those people? They are your classmates, your peers, your neighbors, the members of your church, your fellow students at the local university, and the workers in various companies around town. There is a big secret about *all of those* people, a secret that you should know, a secret that will allow you to be successful.

The majority of everyone around you lack the conviction and motivation to do what you are about to do, or are doing. They may be content with working their Monday through Friday job, picking up their paycheck, and doing whatever it is they do with their weekends. For you, the entrepreneur, those people represent your buying public. What they lack in gumption will turn out to benefit you. If you can figure out exactly what they need and deliver it to them for a moderate cost with a reasonable profit margin for yourself, there is no question you will be phenomenally successful.

If you are interested in making big bucks, you should really know a few things about how to "make the big bucks."

As mentioned, anytime you are working for someone else, you are limiting yourself in time and money. Remember, you can only work a limited number of hours and your employer will offer you only so much money. This completely caps what you can do and how much money you can make.

Another important idea about making "big money" is this: In order to make serious money, you have to develop a product that you can sell on the open market. This product can be a song, a book, a software program most businesses *must have*; it cannot be something that involves your constant attention. Another way to think about this is that you want to develop your product one time, be able to replicate it easily, and then sell it many, many times.

If you do a good job putting all of this in place, you will be able to enjoy a nice income for a long time. Maybe even for the rest of your life.

Setting up a project that will give you income and then basically run itself without your input is going to take work. This work involves imagination, dedication, and perseverance. The term for this is "hard work." It is hard, but once accomplished, it is very rewarding. Especially if your project begins providing you with a good, solid monthly income. Even if it is a minimal income, as long as it is steady, you will do okay. After all, if you have five projects all going at the same time and each is providing $500 a month, that is $2500 in monthly income.

Now, imagine if you will, say eight different projects bringing in an average of $7000 each. This would give you a monthly income of $56,000. Your annual pay will reach about $672,000.

You should be able to live on that.

Many entrepreneurs became rich after creating something from very little. The key is to figure out what you can do to create a flow of money that will come your way and keep coming.

Now, remember that you not only have to develop the product, you have to figure out a couple of other things. One is marketing — how will you let the world know you have this great idea ready to sell that everyone must have? Advertising is a challenge, in the best of times. It can also very expensive. Accordingly, you are going to have to plan well for advertising costs if you want to make money with your project.

The second daunting problem is delivery. How do you plan to get all those widgets to the paying customer? They are not going to get there on their own... So, just how are you going to get your idea, your product, into the hands of your paying customers?

The concept of figuring all this out—well—as I mentioned, is referred to as work. Once you have everything in place, you can sit back a little and relax, to a point. You are still going to have to manage your business, but once you have figured out exactly what you want to do to make money, you will have completed the lion's share of the work.

Chapter 17 – Keep your nose clean; you must have integrity

In order to be successful, you have to do the right thing. You must be a good person. You have to meet the requirements of all those old clichés. It might seem trite, but in order for you to do well, you have to help others. It is a fact of life.

Life is truly not a "me" thing, although some really believe it is so. Sometimes, it takes a long time for a person to realize helping others is very rewarding. It is true that to give is better than to receive. Really, there is such a thing in life as karma.

Abraham Lincoln said, "I never had a policy; I've just tried to do my very best each and every day." It seems like a good policy—doing your best every day. At the end of the day, you can, and will, feel good about yourself.

To jump from Lincoln's time to our time, Congressman J.C. Watts perhaps put it best when he said, "Character is doing the right thing when nobody's looking. There are too many people who think that the only thing that's right is to get by, and the only thing that's wrong is to get caught." This is a sad situation.

Unfortunately, there are many today who live by the last part of Congressmen Watts' statement. Many high school students as well as college students believe cheating is only wrong if someone catches you. If students were to spend as much time doing the job right in the first place, they would not have to cheat to make the grade. And oh, by the way, they really did not make the grade and it will show up later on their jobs when they perform inadequately.

Those who cheat will never know the emotional high of working for a goal and achieving it— actually making it to the finish line. They will never know that inner feeling of pride; to them, satisfaction is a foreign concept.

Cheating is something not limited to school. There are many ways to cheat in life and once caught, some cheaters are unable to fix their situation. Hang with the wrong people, get arrested, and see how well that fits in with the plans for the rest of your life. Fudge on your taxes and then try explaining it to the IRS. Think you can shoplift? Think again.

Now, let's talk about something really heavy.

Drinking and drugs.

Drinking is the drug that is internationally accepted as legal, at least if you are of age as defined by state or local laws. Illicit drugs are not. Still, both can get a young person in a world of hurt after an arrest.

Drugs—don't mess with illegal substances, period. There are many illegal substances available to tempt people of all ages. You guys (the generation this book targets) are wizards with the Internet. Go Google "drug use photos before and after." If what you see does not scare you away from doing illicit drugs forever, well, I hate to say this, but you may have a serious disconnect somewhere in your brain.

I don't write these things to be mean; what the paragraph above states is simple fact.

Regarding drinking—don't drink underage. If you do and you're caught, again, you are going to have a lot of doors slammed in your face when it comes to the career choices of your future. When I went through college, after I became legal to drink, I kept sight of the end game. I was in college to study and pursue a professional position in aviation. Those goals kept me on track. Consequently, I limited my consumption of beer to Friday nights and Saturdays. Sunday through Thursday was for serious studying.

Think about it.

If you really want to be successful, holding alcohol to weekends is no big deal. You will have plenty of time to drink later. Additionally, you will probably be in a better position to enjoy it.

Those who are successful in life, usually have a good plan. If you are going off to college, or you are in college, perhaps you should limit your drinking to Friday and Saturday nights and use the rest of your time for serious study.

When some young people go off to college or get away from their parent's home for the first time, their sudden freedom may overwhelm them. No longer do they have boundaries as to what they can or cannot do. They don't have to ask anyone's permission. This is where parents get their final grade as to the job they did in raising their children. Young adults who instinctively know what to do and do the right thing award their parents with a final grade of "A."

Some children really get into trouble. Sometimes it is the kind of trouble that cannot be undone. Increasingly, it is not the parents' fault. In some instances, blame falls squarely on the shoulders of the young person. We all have the ability to make decisions; it is the nature of those the decisions which define us as the people we become.

This chapter deals with something many prefer not to address which is, namely, playing by the rules. Some will say rules are meant to be broken, but the truth of the matter is this; it is far easier to swim with the tide than to fight it.

Here's the first rule you need, and you really should take care to pay attention.

Rule 1) Do the right thing. Play fair. If you follow the rules as you should, you shouldn't get into trouble. Don't try to cheat to make a cheap buck.

Integrity is an almost forgotten concept. If you live your life with integrity, you will be successful. Everyone around you will recognize what you are doing and they will do their best to help you achieve your goals, because when you are successful, those around you are, too. Conversely, they will also see right through anyone lacking integrity; if you are a fraud, or people see you as such, you can bet your last dollar they will do everything possible to help you fail. A corollary to this rule is Rule 2).

Rule 2) Seriously, treat others, as you would like to be treated. No one likes being treated badly; and if you treat others badly, it is going to come around full circle and bite you where you sit.

Rule 3) There is more than one way to make money and you don't have to have job to get it.

The truth is you can make money without having a job (but holding a job helps). There are many other things you can do to generate living funds and you should know it is actually beneficial to develop different methods for creating income. This leads to another important rule and you should follow this one as well as you can.

Rule 4) Develop as many ways possible to make money on a steady basis. If you have money coming in from different directions, if one of those sources of income fails, you lose only part of your income instead of *all* of your income. If your only source of income is your paycheck, you will be in a lot of trouble should you lose your job.

Rule 5) Keep at least three months' salary in reserve just in case you do lose your job. This is a good rule, if you can follow it. At the beginning of your working life, it might be hard to do, but after becoming established, keeping this much in a reserve fund might be just the ticket you need for finding another job or another income-producing project.

Rule 6) Find a job that pays at least 10 percent more than what you need, or learn to live on 90 percent of what you make. If this is not possible, then remember Rule 3) and make certain the total of all of your jobs or sources of income will give you that 10 percent margin over your budget requirements. Save the 10 percent.

Rule 7) Keep very detailed and clean financial records. If you do, you will know where you started, where you are, and where you are headed — financial bliss or total financial rack and ruin. The former is good, and you want to avoid the latter.

By knowing where you are, you can make a better plan for getting where you want to go. In a manner of speaking, good financial data gives you a visual picture of your current situation and allows you to figure out what to do to make more money and increase your wealth. Without the information, it is very hard to plan.

Additionally, good financial records can help out — a lot — should the IRS come calling. If you have good, detailed records and you have been living your life in accordance with Rule 1) above, you will have no trouble answering an IRS agent's questions.

Rule 8) *Jake's[1] Corollary:* Never stay out late. Nothing good ever happens after midnight.

Rule 9) Pick a career you really enjoy. If you really like your job, you can work a whole lifetime and never feel as though you went to work a day in your life.

Rule 10) Have fun. Whatever you end up doing while making a living, if you are having fun doing it, you will never feel as though you are working.

---

[1] Jake is a famous fighter pilot of F-4 and A-4 experience who has passed down many incredible jewels of advice and pearls of wisdom to young people. He has helped shape the lives and careers of thousands of new fighter pilots, airline and corporate pilots, and continues doing so to this day.

We hope this guide was beneficial in giving our young people good ideas on how to manage the possibitlities of their futures.

Please visit www.bluewaterpress.com to check out our other titles and offerings in non-fiction and fiction, from history to novels.

www.ingramcontent.com/pod-product-compliance
Lightning Source LLC
Chambersburg PA
CBHW031645040426
42453CB00006B/215